BOMBER CREW

JACK E. THOMPSON, DFC
Second Edition
With additional material by
Stephen Thompson

© Copyright 2005 Jack E. Thompson
Edited by Stephen Thompson

All rights reserved. No part of this publication may be reproduced, stored in a retrieval system, or transmitted, in any form or by any means, electronic, mechanical, photocopying, recording, or otherwise, without the written prior permission of the author.

Note for Librarians: A cataloguing record for this book is available from Library and Archives Canada at www.collectionscanada.ca/amicus/index-e.html
ISBN 1-4120-6715-4

Printed on paper with minimum 30% recycled fibre. Trafford's print shop runs on "green energy" from solar, wind and other environmentally-friendly power sources.

Offices in Canada, USA, Ireland and UK

This book was published *on-demand* in cooperation with Trafford Publishing. On-demand publishing is a unique process and service of making a book available for retail sale to the public taking advantage of on-demand manufacturing and Internet marketing. On-demand publishing includes promotions, retail sales, manufacturing, order fulfilment, accounting and collecting royalties on behalf of the author.

Book sales for North America and international:
Trafford Publishing, 6E–2333 Government St.,
Victoria, BC v8t 4p4 CANADA
phone 250 383 6864 (toll-free 1 888 232 4444)
fax 250 383 6804; email to orders@trafford.com

Book sales in Europe:
Trafford Publishing (uk) Ltd., Enterprise House, Wistaston Road Business Centre, Wistaston Road, Crewe, Cheshire cw2 7rp UNITED KINGDOM
phone 01270 251 396 (local rate 0845 230 9601)
facsimile 01270 254 983; orders.uk@trafford.com

Order online at:
trafford.com/05-1626

10 9 8 7 6 5 4 3 2

Copyright Jack E. Thompson, 1989

DEDICATION

To the memory of Dr. James Peacock, DFC.

To the surviving members of the crew of "G – George" of 12 Squadron, Wickenby: Jack Chapman, Arnold Cowan, Cal Dagg, Gerald Jones and Ron Smith.

To my wife Dorothy who was there.

Grateful acknowledgment (1st edition) is made:

To Fred Heidman, manager, and staff members of the Parry Sound North Star for their great assistance.

To my friend Bert Weir of Loon Studios, Parry Sound for his artistic contributions and suggestions.

To Jack Dryden of P.S. Printing, Parry Sound for his suggestions, expertise and co-operation.

Cover sign and squadron crest design by Bert Weir.

JACK E. THOMPSON

FOREWORD TO 2005 EDITION

There are many reasons why I have chosen this publishing project, to produce a second edition of my father's 1989 book, *Bomber Crew*. Primary amongst these reasons, there are no longer any new copies from the original printing run, and I think this story deserves to be told to another generation.

My father, Jack Thompson, died on March 12 2003. I believe a re-issue is a fitting tribute, part of a memorial. This year I have had the distinct pleasure to publish another book, *Reflections Through A Special Lens*, based on my father's material, in this case, a lifetime of black-and-white photography.

In the sixteen intervening years, 1989 to 2005, technological advances have allowed me to "hunt-and-peck" and edit on the fly. My dad used a small electric typewriter, typing quickly with a two finger "hunt-and-peck" method developed over years of newspaper writing and editing. We both could always write easily, albeit with different styles, mine developed through scientific writing, his news writing, both essentially a "just the facts, ma'am" style stripped of embellishment. We have both learned to become story-tellers.

I have replaced the photographs of the original edition with new digital images. I think these will print better today. Some will not since they may be digital images but they are from old material. I have discovered other photographs, not available in 1989, and I have added some of my own photos from a 2005 visit to the United Kingdom.

On May 8, 2005, the 60th anniversary of VE-Day, Victory in Europe Day, I visited what remains of the Wickenby aerodrome in Lincolnshire, England, an eerily *déjà vu* experience as this is the 'drome that features so prominently in this book. This anniversary, it is widely believed, will be the final major celebration of VE-Day, old enemies have become friends and great numbers of the celebrants, the veterans, are not expected to survive until another milestone date is reached. But, "lest we forget ...", World War II remains an important hallmark, and, hopefully, a major lesson in the history of western civilization. My generation's lives have been easy compared to the experiences of these boys. I use the word "boys" deliberately. My father flew a large military aircraft into enemy territory and led a crew of six other men before he was 21 years old. I do not know whether I could have been capable of the same at the same age. Another reason for this edition at this time.

But, enough about my reasons. Primarily, I think *Bomber Crew* is a very good read and I am pleased to be able to present a fresh edition.

Steve Thompson
Kirkfield, Ontario
June 2005

Jack Thompson in front of living quarters, Wickenby, Lincolnshire, England, 1944

BOMBER CREW

PROLOGUE

Forty-one years after we had said our goodbyes to our faithful Lancaster G - George, to 12 Squadron friends and to Wickenby, six of the original seven of us were together again in September, 1985. Our reunion was held in Sarnia at the spacious home of our rear-gunner Cal. The only sad note in our three-day gathering was the absence of our bomb-aimer Jim who died of cancer in 1962. We drank a toast to Jim's memory, talked about him for a few minutes, then got on with the reunion.

This was a time for the living, for the six of us who had not only survived the war but also the peace that followed. Forty-one years is a long time for the separation of such a group as closely-knit as we had been but we gathered up the years, thrust them aside and immediately resumed our former camaraderie.

Cal was the one who promoted and organized this historic (as far as we were concerned) get-together. Ron flew from England and Arnold from Edmonton; Chappy drove from Ottawa, Jonesy from nearby Chatham and I from Parry Sound. We six, four of whom were retired and one semi-retired, had worked as civilians for forty years. Instead of the kids we had been years before, with the exception of Arnold who was older than rest of us, we were now experienced old-timers as far as life was concerned. Naturally we looked older than we did in 1944 but I felt, and I think the others did, that we were still the same people basically as we had been in those long-ago days of comradeship. On that significant weekend our memories were revived as we talked and looked at photographs and we all, in our minds, revisited Wickenby and re-lived those stress-filled hours .....

This book was merely in the thinking stage then, and now, three years later in September 1988, following a second crew reunion at Cal's again, the first work on the project is beginning.

There are several reasons for writing the book. One has been a personal desire of mine during these 40-odd years. But as is the case with many personal desires, no matter how strong, procrastination is a deadly barrier to accomplishment.

There is no question that our crew reunions helped to motivate me and so did a suggestion I heard on CFRB radio from Bill McVean. Bill's message was, "Everyone should write an autobiography. How else will our children, grandchildren and great-grandchildren know how it was for us?"

This book is, of course, not an autobiography or a biography; it is simply an attempt to describe the short span of a few months during which we seven filled our destined roles together. Although of short duration, these months were perhaps the most significant period in our lives. As such I think they warrant a written record for our descendants.

Another reason for the book was a challenge thrown out by Chappy, our irrepressible wireless operator who, at the 1988 reunion said, "I don't see how you can write a book about us. We didn't do anything!" Of course he didn't really mean that literally. I'm sure that what he meant was that the annals of our operational experiences were not exciting enough to provide interesting reading. Certainly, compared with some of the many books that have been written about the war in the air our tale may indeed be dull.

We didn't come limping home on two or three engines with the aircraft shot to pieces and crew members dead or wounded.

We didn't wind up ditching in the English Channel or the North Sea and floating about in a rubber dinghy for several days.

We didn't get shot down and have to bail out over occupied Europe.

None of these dramatic, book-creating episodes happened to us. We simply breezed through with no great problems, completed our tour of operations in jig time and that was it. But through it all we did have enough adrenalin-creating happenings to keep us far from being bored.

I think this is the essence of the book. Many other crews must have had a similar tour to ours but these are the ones never heard about --

those who simply did the job to the best of their ability and returning safely and in unheroic fashion.

One note regarding the pages which follow: Much of the book has been written in the first person which has given undue prominence to the author who was, after all, just one member of a seven-man crew. The original intention was not to emphasize the pilot's role and his thoughts and observations. But, since this was not a work of fiction, it was impossible at this time to explore the minds of the crew members and to report their thoughts and feelings with accuracy. There may well be errors and certainly omissions. More than 40 years is a long time to preserve details in the mind when the only written reference is the terse record in a pilot's log book.

1985 & 1991 Crew Reunions, Sarnia, Ontario and Royal Canadian Legion, Parry Sound, Ontario

JACK E. THOMPSON

CHAPTER 1

Ron had dumped the landing gear and flaps and we were coasting in, a steady 120 MPH showing on the airspeed indicator. The final approach to the end of the runway was nicely lined up and I was listening to the short, terse announcements from arriving aircraft as their skippers called up to receive landing instructions.

I glanced over at Ron. He grinned back. We were doing our thing that we had done many times before but this time it was different. This time it was a particularly happy occasion shadowed slightly by overtones of sadness. We knew that we would never be doing this again together. The rest of the crew in their various locations in the big flying machine were silent, all seven of us sharing the elation and, at the same time, the finality of our time together.

My concentration on the approach was suddenly broken by the finely-modulated English-accented voice which interrupted the steady flow of communications between air and ground.

"Careful, Tommy, careful!"

The message coming through my headphones made me chuckle with delight.

"That's that old bugger Frank Watt," I told the others.

Frank's message was a warm and personal acknowledgement of the particular significance of our imminent touch-down and also let us knows that he too had returned safely from the operation. Trust him to ignore radio procedure rules on this important occasion for both of us. I was too busy to make a reply as we swished down over the end of the runway.

And what an important occasion it was! Our two crews, with this flight, completed the final operation of our tours and could now look forward to a period of much more relaxed living. No longer were we faced with the knowledge that our next trip aloft might be our final goodbye to life.

We landed and taxied clear of the runway continuing along the perimeter strip to the hard-stand where we shut down the engines.

We'd made it! It was a smiling, joking crew who carted their parachutes and other equipment to the door and descended the ladder one by one to terra firma. An M.T. section truck was standing by to carry us to the briefing hut where debriefing would be the final formality of our tour.

The date was November 6, 1944, a cheerful blue-sky day, unusual for England at this time of year. Over Germany, bright sunlight and a blue sky had also predominated but its smiling innocence had not misled us. Unlike Irving Berlin's "Blue skies smiling at me" the German sky was anything but the optimistic description in Berlin's next line, "Nothing but blue skies do I see".

Blue the sky may have been but its beauty was marred by myriads of black puffs from exploding anti-aircraft shells. The air corridor we travelled had become a deadly sea of bursting charges.

Our target, Gelsenkirchen, was in the heavy industrial section of Germany, the Ruhr, known to bomber crews as "Happy Valley". Looking at the countless disintegrating smoke clusters from flak bursts drifting by on each side of us it seemed as though the route had been chosen to expose us to the most anti-aircraft fire over the longest possible period.

But as someone said during our first days on the squadron, "You don't have to worry about the black puffs, they're already done." And this was true of course but, where there was a great concentration of visible anti-aircraft fire, there were bound to be many as yet unexploded shells whizzing by just ready to demolish an aircraft or at least inflict considerable damage. This was certainly one of the heaviest concentrations of ack-ack we had seen on any of our daylight trips and it continued without let-up for miles. To quote a popular description among crews, "The flak was thick enough to get out and walk on". And a lot of the bursts seemed to be zeroing in at our height.

This was emphasized in a most drastic way. Another Lancaster had been flying for some time just a few hundred yards ahead and to starboard of us. Suddenly the Lanc disappeared! All that remained where a moment before it had been flying was a small cloud of black smoke and some odd bits and pieces spinning through the air.

At one moment seven men in a big aircraft, then poof! everything was gone. Apparently a direct hit had exploded its bomb load. This was one of the times during the tour, and on our last trip too, that we were in intimate contact with the cold, hard realities of war.

"Did you see that?" Ron asked me, "Poor sods didn't have a chance."

I could only nod my head in mute agreement and think to myself with the brutal philosophy to which we had grown accustomed, "Better them than us."

Within a few seconds our close call was underlined when Jimmie called up from the nose that he had almost been hit by a piece of flak! He'd been lying prone in his bomb release position working out his calculations for the bomb-run, referring to the data on his clipboard. Suddenly the board bounced up in his face. After the first moment of bewilderment he realized the corner of the board had been clipped by a fragment. Later we discovered a neat hole in the Perspex nose but we couldn't find the piece of flak which, like an enraged wasp, had sought out the one man who would inflict the damage on its home.

Before Jim had much time to dwell on his good fortune we settled down to the bomb-run, dropped our load and skedaddled out of that very unfriendly bit of German real estate.

Home ground had never seemed more desirable. Nothing could go wrong now on this our last trip -- we hoped! And as it turned out nothing did go wrong as we droned our way back to our English base as quickly as possible.

I'm afraid we were all so relieved and happy after we climbed out of the aircraft that we didn't really bid our faithful Lancaster "G" George a proper goodbye. We just pulled away in the truck from the big bird without so much as a backward glance leaving her standing stalwart and alone. It was the last time any of us would see her, the aircraft that carried us successfully through 19 of our more than 30 operations.

The sergeants' mess was the scene that night of our celebration. We had lived through a tour of operations that had included a variety of targets. We had taken part in the "greatest air operation in history" as the bombing of Caen in support of Allied troops had been called. We had flown over France, Belgium and Holland to hit targets of strategic importance in these German-occupied countries. We had bombed targets in Germany's industrial Ruhr and also made much deeper penetrations of the Third Reich.

Some of the operations had been short, relatively easy excursions. Most of these were made in daylight. Other forays against the enemy had lasted for as much as eight hours with the resultant nervous tension kept at peak through the long night.

We had several close encounters and many imagined ones with German night-fighters.

We had undergone enough fright, enough tension, enough "adventure" as well as some exhilaration and had seen enough awe-inspiring sights to last us a lifetime -- and all in a little more than four months.

And at the party that night we had drunk and sang and talked about it all with a feeling of sheer relief so different from the artificial bravado paraded at other mess parties. This celebration was held in the N.C.O.'s mess because most members of the crew were not allowed in the officers' mess. Jim the bomb-aimer and I were the only commissioned officers among the seven of us at the time. This ruling about messes was military tradition which we resented but were unable to do anything about. It seemed to us that, since we all flew together facing exactly the same hazards and performing our duties as a team, we should be allowed to eat and socialize together as well while on the station. Of course we did when off the base.

Anyway we had a grand party along with Frank Watt's crew and a third crew skippered by a Scot named appropriately enough Jock. We had all finished on the same day, apparently due to an administrative foul-up and the C.O. was not happy at losing his three most experienced crews all at once. But we didn't mind. That was his problem. We'd all made it, we were all happy, and we celebrated.

Just a few days later we left Wickenby, our station in the flatlands of Lincolnshire, for the last time. The five Canadians in the crew were on their way home. Apparently by this time there was a surplus of air crew in Britain. Chappy and Ron, the wireless operator and flight engineer, both English types, were posted to other stations.

JACK E. THOMPSON

The timing of our departure could not have been better. Four of us, three from Ontario and one from Quebec, made it home for Christmas Day, 1944. Our navigator, Arnold, did not quite make it because he lived in Edmonton.

I don't know how the others felt as the war continued in Europe for another six months. I was pleased to be home but, at the same time, felt strangely lost in Canada. Most of all I regretted not being in England on V-E Day, that great day in history which saw the end of the Nazi empire and which all of the Allied servicemen and women helped to bring about.

Crew of Lancaster "C – Charlie", 12 Squadron
Wickenby 1944

L to R: Jimmy Reid, rear gunner, Nick Nicholson, flight engineer, Gilly Gill, wireless operator, Frank Watt, pilot, Sid Palmer, navigator, Goldie Golding, mid-upper gunner, Butch Wellstead, bomb aimer

CHAPTER 2

A World War II bomber crew was a team of highly trained specialists prepared to play a deadly game for the dual prizes of success and survival.

In spite of the urgent need for aircrew, the Royal Canadian Air Force ensured that its pilots, navigators, bomb aimers, wireless operators and air gunners went into action as well prepared as possible. My training as a pilot took one and one-half years beginning with tiny single-engined aircraft and progressing to four-engined monsters.

Navigators spent probably an equivalent length of time in ground school and practical flying exercises. Bomb aimers trained for months perfecting their sighting and releasing of hundreds of practice bombs and learning all the intricacies of setting various factors on their bomb sights. They also learned to handle the .303 Browning machine guns standard in the nose turret of bomber aircraft.

Practice, practice and more practice was the only method by which wireless operators became adept and speedy in sending and receiving Morse code. They also were required to understand all radio, r/t and intercom equipment on board and to effect emergency repairs. As well they qualified as air gunners and could take over any of the gun positions.

Air gunners fired thousands of rounds at drogues towed by

another aircraft. They learned deflections, how to control gun turrets and how to service their weapons. Their Browning .303s were our only defence.

Crewing up was a very hit-or-miss affair. Imagine a huge hall filled with a motley assortment of pilots, navigators, bomb aimers, wireless operators and air gunners. All had been through the full round of training courses. We were as qualified to begin melding together as a crew as we were ever going to be. We had to trust to luck that we were all compatible.

The word went out, "Get crewed up", the signal for strangers to meet and begin to build a team. There was no time to have conversations or ask questions the answers to which might help to justify a choice.

In our case we were lucky with our selections, actually my choices, since I would be the skipper. I noticed a short, older chap wearing a navigator's wing and thought to myself, "He looks capable and serious-minded, just the sort who should really know his stuff." And so we acquired Arnold and thanked our lucky stars many times in the future when his maturity and navigational expertise kept us out of trouble.

I was approached by two gunners, Cal, small and slight, Jonesy, tall and stocky. "We'd like to be together in the same crew," they told me. They looked eager and somehow business-like. I said, "Sure", and then we were four. Two more to go and the choices quickly dwindling.

A pilot officer bomb aimer seemed to be standing quietly by himself amid the hubbub. I was a sergeant at the time but, after a moment's hesitation I asked him if he would like to join our crew and he agreed readily. I don't know why Jim had been left among the last to be crewed up but I suspect it may have been his officer's rank that made a number of sergeant pilots less than anxious to have him in their crew.

Once again we were lucky. It turned out that Jim had not passed as a navigator and had remustered to bomb aimer. As well as a highly capable and dedicated bomb aimer he was also able to offer a lot of assistance to Arnold with navigation.

We still didn't have a wireless operator until two RAF flight-sergeant W/OPs suddenly appeared. Apparently they had been late arrivals. We were fortunate once again when Chappy became the sixth member of our crew. He was already a veteran W/OP/AG having over 1,000 flying hours many of which he picked up as an instructor. He was also the only Englishman in our bunch. Chappy told me later that when he and his chum George Adcock arrived, only two crews were short of wireless operators. The pair flipped a coin and Chappy came to us while George joined the crew of my best friend, Wally Simpson. Now we were six, a full crew until such time as we started flying four-engined aircraft and were joined by a flight engineer.

I should point out that we five members of the Royal Canadian Air Force were attached to the Royal Air Force and served with the RAF all the time we were in England. This was very common. Twenty-five per cent of the RAF was made up of Canadians.

Before we go any further it's time for introductions: Our talented navigator was Arnold Cowan, age 33, an old guy by aircrew standards. In fact Arnold was initially rejected for aircrew because he was "too old". He joined the RCAF in 1942 as a pharmacist with the rank of sergeant and, two days later, was told he was now "young enough" for aircrew. He immediately remustered and became the lowest of the low, an AC2 (Aircraftsman Second Class) which is the rank in which we all started.

Arnold grew up, attended school and worked around Calgary and Edmonton for a while before enrolling in the University of Alberta. He graduated as a pharmacist. Arnold was married and I think it was his solid, no-nonsense, dependable look that attracted me to him that day we crewed up. Just looking at him I felt that he would have a lot to offer -- and a great interest in survival.

Jim Peacock was, initially, the only officer in our crew which made no difference to him or to the rest of us. He was immediately one of the boys. He was our bomb aimer, the one member of the crew who completed the job that we were sent out to do. He lined us up on the bombing run and pressed the button at the right moment to send our destructive load hurtling earthwards. He handled his job conscientiously and with great precision.

One of Jim's most interesting traits, which the rest of us respected and did not scoff at, was his strong, almost obsessive superstition. He quietly made sure that no one in the crew ever took a third light; his aversion to the number 13 was so great that we didn't fly a thirteenth operation but rather number 12A. When it came time to have a bunch of little bombs painted on the nose of our aircraft to denote the number of operations flown, Jim said, "No. Everything has been going along o.k. so let's not change anything now." We didn't push it so George, our Lancaster, never did receive any adornment.

Our witty, wise-cracking, entertaining wireless operator/air gunner was Jack Chapman who we called Chappy. An Englishman, Chappy was suddenly thrust among a collection of Canadians but survived the experience very nicely always giving more than he got.

He came to us with loads of flying experience, far more than any of the rest of us, and this in itself made him invaluable. After he graduated and received his wing Chappy was posted to an Advanced Observers Flying Unit as a staff instructor. This was a strong indication of his expertise. He was also a flight-sergeant, a rank above all of us but Jim Peacock at that time.

Cal and Jonesy were our protectors, our air gunners who shared six Browning .303 machine guns, four in the "tail-end Charlie" turret with Cal, two in the mid-upper position handled by Jonesy. They joined the crew as fresh and eager as two juniors who had just been drafted by the NHL. Cal Dagg came from Sarnia, Gerald Jones from not far from there in the Chatham area. Cal was a little guy, cocky and, although the expression had not been coined in those days, gung-ho. Jonesy was a tall, well-built young man, quieter than Cal in demeanour but full of life and raring to go. They had trained together and looked forward to being in the same crew. Cal's size made him a natural for the cramped rear turret.

For their pilot these guys were saddled with me, Jack Thompson, known among the crew as Tommy, from Peterborough. I managed to learn something about flying an aeroplane in Canada starting out on a ski-equipped Fleet Finch, a little biplane, and progressing to twin-engined Ansons. The latter pointed me in the direction of bombers rather than single-engined fighters and I was pleased with this. I don't think I would have made a good fighter pilot.

In England I trained on twin-engined Oxfords before crewing up. In my opinion my main attribute as a pilot was instrument flying. I had received an excellent grounding in this from a very tough demanding instructor in Canada. When my Oxford instructor in England took me up for instrument practice he called it off after the first few minutes. "You don't need this," he said, "Let's go low flying."

We added one more member to the crew after we had completed

OTU (Operational Training Unit) but that is another part of this story.

An OTU in England's Midlands became our home for a month and a half where we acquired about 80 hours of flying as a crew. We also grew to know each other and a camaraderie began to emerge which would strengthen as the months went by and the total dependence on each other's capabilities would become acknowledged.

Our introduction to flying as a crew was a greater transition for me than for any of the others all of whom had spent their flying training days in groups within the aircraft. My flying training had been carried out with an instructor or alone or occasionally with another student pilot. Now, suddenly, there were six of us on board and I was responsible for five other lives.

It must have been very boring for the boys while I received instruction and practiced circuits and bumps on an aircraft which seemed like a monster after the little twins flown previously. The aeroplanes we flew at OTU were Wellingtons, familiarly known as Wimpies. Although having only two engines they were a large aircraft with a wing span of about 80 feet. At one time the Wellington was the RAF's front-line bomber. It was strongly built and although slow, gave a good account of itself.

As I mentioned, having the responsibility for five others instead of just for myself was a new feeling. But it was also surprisingly reassuring to have some companionship while stooging about the sky on long cross-country training flights.

The most reassuring thing of all, and the greatest change for me, was having a navigator. It was absolutely wonderful to have someone tell me what course to fly, when to change course, when to start letting down and to be able to call up and say, "Where are we?" and get a quick answer.

It was a whole new experience to climb through cloud and break out into the clear. We never did this in earlier pilot training. Climbing up was fine but when you were above the clouds you didn't know what was below so a blind descent was fraught with danger. There was no instrument in the cockpit that told you whether or not there were hills below those clouds and if it was o.k. to slide down.

But now all that was different! Now Arnold's radar could tell him exactly where we were at any given moment while flying over England. With that knowledge he could then tell me whether it was safe to descend through cloud.

I'll have to admit that the first time we did this I was searching very hard for that ground below, hoping we would be well above it as we broke out of the overcast. We crept down through several thousand feet of cloud which is like being encased in thick fog. I was watching the altimeter unwind - 4000 feet, 3000, 2500, 2000 – it was starting to get too close for comfort. Suddenly the light greyness around us darkened and we broke free of the last wispy tendrils of cloud to see the good earth some 1500 feet below.

It was a great feeling! The radar had proven itself and Arnold had proven himself. After this demonstration I had complete confidence in our navigation system and our navigator.

Two events are outstanding in my mind from our OTU days and I'm sure the second one in particular is well remembered by all the crew.

The first one was an encounter with icing, that dread situation which has caused many an aircraft to crash. We realized that ice was starting to form on the Wellington while on a cross-country training flight. We were descending through cloud at the time and I suddenly noticed that I couldn't see through the windshield.

We knew that warmer air at a lower height would prevent further ice build-up and would melt some of the deadly casing forming on the wings. Too much ice and the lift characteristics of the wings would be destroyed and we would plunge earthward out of control.

In order to steepen our angle of descent without getting into an uncontrolled dive I put down flaps and undercarriage and throttled back. We made a fairly rapid descent and experienced no difficulties with control. But the windscreen hadn't lost its solid coating of ice by the time we arrived back at the airport.

I slid open the tiny side window and was able to see out to the side and slightly ahead. I had to keep sliding the nose to starboard in order to get glimpses of the runway. This was the way we made our approach and landing, which, as it turned out, worked out quite well. It was a hairy experience and it was the only time we faced this problem.

The second event was equally hairy but was over too quickly to cause us much alarm. We were doing circuits and bumps when we made our one and only crash landing. During a landing I dropped in from too high above the runway causing us to take quite a bounce. Immediately I jammed the throttles ahead to get up flying speed and go around again. But the engines failed to respond with enough power! We were staggering along a few feet above the runway but not gaining any forward speed or height! The long strip of macadam was quickly shortening and I could see we weren't going to make it. "Put the wheels down," I yelled to Jim who was sitting in the right hand seat. I yanked the throttles back and we sank down on the tarred surface of the runway with no great impact. We had the petrol and engines switched off and slid along with a great scraping sound for a short distance, then stopped.

It was such a surprise to everyone that we sat there for a moment until someone shouted, "Let's get the hell out of here!" Then our reflexes numbed by the suddenness and strangeness of our landing took over and we climbed out through several exits very quickly and got well away from the potential fire hazard.

As it turned out no fire developed, the blades of the two propellers were badly twisted and the belly of the aircraft damaged. It was an exciting few moments and we never did find out why the aircraft couldn't climb. The undercarriage was probably also damaged because the wheels hadn't come down in time -- but it was worth a try.

We completed OTU, had some leave, and eventually headed for our first experience with heavy bombers and a further welding together of our crew of six, shortly to become a group of seven.

Crew of Lancaster "G – George", 12 Squadron

Wickenby 1944

L to R: Ron Smith, flight engineer, Gerald Jones, mid-upper gunner, Jack Thompson, pilot, Cal Dagg, rear gunner, Jack Chapman, wireless operator, Arnold Cowan, navigator. Squatting in front: Jim Peacock, bomb aimer.

CHAPTER 3

Two major changes took place with our introduction to heavy conversion unit.

The first and by far the most important was the completion of our crew with the addition of a flight engineer. Now we were seven, all highly trained specialists, a collection of individuals thrown together by chance like the cast of dice. We original six had grown accustomed to each other by this time, beginning to forge the strong bonds which would link us together for a lifetime.

Now we had to assimilate a new partner in the company. With Ron this was no problem. Perhaps it was for him but certainly not for the rest of us for, like Chappy, he was an Englishman being thrown into the company of a bunch of Canadians.

Ron Smith, a native of the Manchester area, with a quiet disposition but certainly not lacking a sense of humour, joined us at heavy conversion unit. Ron was a highly qualified technician who knew and understood the mechanical, electrical and hydraulic systems of our big, sophisticated aircraft.

With his arrival and our switch to four-engined machines I suddenly realized that we were flying real top-of-the-line warplanes. I was actually going to be in charge of an aircraft that required the services of a flight engineer to keep all the technical details under control! In addition to doing pre-flight checks and constantly monitoring the multitude of gauges, Ron also helped me with the flying by raising and lowering the undercarriage and flaps, starting up and shutting down engines among other things. He was a welcome completion of our crew and proved his worth and competence on numerous occasions.

The second major change was the switch from twin-engined aircraft to monsters with four engines which seemed like quite a jump and I know I faced the prospect with some apprehension. As well as having four engines, our training Halifaxes were very large machines. The wings stretched outward from the fuselage almost 50 feet on each side and the Halifax was about 70 feet long, equivalent to a good-sized ranch-style bungalow.

Halifaxes were front-line operational bombers and, as such, were good performers. Why we did our conversion on them rather than the Lancasters we would be flying I don't know. Perhaps it was because the Hally was a very easy aircraft to land. Or perhaps Lancs were all being used operationally and were not available.

We had begun our course on May 25th at a time of great expectation in England. By this time everyone in the country knew that the cross-Channel invasion of Europe was not far off, but of course, the date and location were well-guarded secrets.

On the morning of June 6th we were scheduled for an appointment with a fighter for practice. While we were getting ready we were electrified by the announcement that D-Day had begun. We heard General Dwight Eisenhower, Supreme Allied Commander ETO, telling the world over the radio that the first landings had been carried out on the French coast.

Imagine the excitement this news generated! This was the long-awaited invasion that, if successful, would signal the beginning of the end of the years of war in Europe. Thousands of ships of all descriptions, bearing a mighty army of men and equipment, and droves of aircraft were zeroing in on a number of French coastal areas.

And here we were, just a short distance away in air miles from the epic scene and unable to get even a glimpse! Instead we were heading out on a routine training flight while this history-making event was taking place. Even when airborne we were not able to sneak south for a peek. There was a line in southern England beyond which no unauthorized aircraft were allowed to pass.

We missed D-Day by a month but would be making some trips in support of the Allied advance on the continent when we joined our squadron.

I mentioned earlier that the Halifax was an easy aircraft to land. After the final round-out one had to simply pull the control column back strongly and the machine mushed onto the runway. I remember particularly a training session on cross-wind landings which can be nasty if not handled properly. The technique was clearly in my mind a few days later when we arrived back at the aerodrome to find a strong cross-wind blowing across our designated runway. So here goes, I thought; now's your chance to try it out.

Everything went beautifully. We touched down with absolutely no side motion. When we were walking into the flight office I realized the landing had been under observation by my instructor and flight commander. "Nice cross-wind landing, Thompson," remarked the instructor. This was one of the rare occasions upon which I had been commended on my flying ability. It was a heady moment for me, one I have treasured all these years.

One of the drills we were required to practice while we were at the conversion unit dealt with a dinghy. Now these were not sailing dinghies and the drills represented anything but a pleasant day on the water. The drills were to ready us for what we hoped would never happen -- a ditching (landing on the water) in the North Sea or English Channel.

Numerous successful ditchings had been made by bomber crews, we were told, but we had no ambition to add our names to the list of those unfortunates. We were also told that heavy aircraft had been known to float for many minutes but not to count on more than 20 seconds to get clear.

The sessions took place in a fuselage inside a hangar. We all sat in our accustomed places and I called out, "Dinghy, dinghy prepare for ditching" which was supposed to alert the crew to this unfortunate pending manoeuvre. In reality I suppose the message would be more like, "Hey guys we're going to have to go in the drink any minute now so get ready." Anyway, after the signal from the pilot the crew members had to move quickly into their crash positions. Jim and Arnold had to climb up out of the nose section (this was a Halifax fuselage), Cal out of the rear turret and so on until all were sitting on the floor braced for impact

Then I called out "First impact" and, after a pause, "Second impact". After that we all scrambled out of the aircraft as quickly as possible,

Ron and I using the overhead hatch in the cockpit reached by standing on my seat.

Theoretically if all went well and if Jonesy remembered to pull the toggle which released the dinghy and started it inflating, we would scramble down the wing or out of the door into the sea and our salvation, the dinghy. This yellow craft should be bobbing at the end of a rope which had to be released quickly before the whole kit and caboodle was dragged under as the aircraft headed for the bottom.

The dinghy was supposed to be equipped with a couple of paddles and a bit of survival gear. Hardly any prospect, other than being shot down, was more depressing than the thought of ditching in the cold and usually wave-tossed waters.

The author and pilot, Jack Thompson, in the cockpit and at the controls of "G – George"

CHAPTER 4

When we first arrived at Lancaster finishing school, Ron trotted me out where a couple of the big birds were parked.

"I think you're going to like the Lanc, Tommy," he told me and proceeded to give me a conducted tour of the aircraft which was representative of the machine we would be flying against the enemy.

My first impression of the famed Lancaster was of a big bird of prey crouched and ready to spring into the air. The massive under-carriage appeared like great talons and the dihedral, the up-bend in the wing beginning just past the inner engine, gave the Lanc a rakish, devil-may-care appearance. While massive in size it seemed sleek and streamlined in comparison with the more boxy Halifaxes we had been flying.

And we soon found out that the Lanc's eager-to-fly appearance was no misrepresentation. This was an aeroplane! Its four great Rolls Royce Merlin engines hurled it from the runway on takeoff and provided the power for steep turns, steep climbs and the famous Lancaster corkscrew (more about that later). It could perform well on three engines and many a Lanc returned safely from an operation with only two engines keeping it aloft.

There is no question that the Avro Lancaster was the finest bomber by far operating out of England. The aircraft's great power and superb flying characteristics made it Bomber Command's most potent weapon. The Lanc's carrying capacity became legendary. An ordinary bomb load could weigh seven and one-half tons but modified Lancs carried as much as 22,000 pounds on special operations.

A full load of petrol, 2,154 gallons, would allow a Lanc to range a little more than 2500 miles with 7,000 pounds of bombs on board. A 12,000 pound bomb load cut the maximum flying distance to 1,730 miles.

And even with the bomb-bay stuffed with 15,000 pounds of armament, the aircraft was no slouch when it came to speed. Its maximum speed with such a load was 275 MPH at 15,000 feet. Cruising speed under the same conditions was 200 MPH

The much-vaunted U.S. Flying Fortress, which was about the same size as the Lancaster, did not begin to compare with the British plane in performance. Fortresses were heavily armour-plated for protection against fighters and could only carry about 1/5th of the weight of bombs compared with the Lanc. We didn't envy this armour-plating but we also didn't envy their daylight raids deep into Germany during which they needed every bit of protection they could get from the German fighters which swarmed like iron filings attracted to a magnet.

The Lancaster was described by Bomber Command's chief, Sir Arthur Harris, as "the greatest single factor in the winning of the war". Although he was no doubt somewhat prejudiced, the British government must have realized the Lanc's great impact in the war effort because 7,377 Lancasters were built, several hundred of these by Victory Aircraft at Malton, Ontario. Statistics show that:

> Lancasters used 228 million gallons of petrol during operations.
>
> The 608,612 tons of bombs dropped by Lancasters represented 63.8 per cent of all bombs dropped by Bomber Command.
>
> Lancs also unloaded 51,513,106 incendiaries.

The Avro Lancaster was a big, beautiful, totally successful bomber. Its wing span measured 102 feet and its length was just six inches short of 70 feet. Ron and I in our seats in the cockpit were suspended almost 20 feet above the ground.

We had our short course on Lancs, about 12 hours flying time, during which I think we all came to admire this magnificent machine. Ron, of course, during his engineer's training was already familiar with the aircraft. I found that the machine, in spite of its size, was extremely responsive to the controls and to the power of its four great Merlins.

One day an instructor showed us the Lancaster Corkscrew, a manoeuvre devised to throw off the aim of an attacking fighter. The instructor suddenly pushed the control column hard ahead and we pitched into a steep dive. Within seconds he pulled the nose up and flipped the ailerons so we were into a climbing turn, then a roll to the other while continuing to climb and back into a steep dive.

This was all supposed to be accompanied by a running commentary from the pilot, "diving port, rolling, climbing starboard, diving starboard, rolling, climbing port etc." repeated for as long as the corkscrew continued. This dialogue was to alert the gunners to the quick changes in attitude so they would not become disoriented. The Lancaster was the only bomber aircraft able to carry out the manoeuvre and could do so even with a bomb load.

As were many other Royal Air Force planes, Lancasters were painted in camouflage colours. The lower part of the fuselage and bottom of the wings were black to make the aircraft merge into the darkness of the night if seen from below. All of the upper surfaces were patterned drab brown and green to help hide the aircraft against the browns and greens of the earth far below during daylight hours.

Whether the paint job was very effective as camouflage we never did know but certainly we didn't stand out in the sky like the silvery glitter of the U.S. Fortresses and Liberators.

When we had completed 12 hours on a Lancaster we were deemed ready and able to begin operational flying. By this time we had drawn even closer together as a team and as friends. We knew everything about our job in theory. Soon we would be tested.

Only two items of significance had occurred at the conclusion of our short Lancaster orientation -- my commission as a pilot officer came through and we learned where we would be posted.

Wickenby was the name of our new station and there we would become members of 12 Squadron. The very low number of our squadron was indicative of its time-honoured background. Formed during World War I, our squadron was one of the oldest in the Royal Air Force.

Wickenby was located in the flat, windswept county of Lincolnshire about 10 miles from the historic City of Lincoln which became one of the principal cities of the Roman conquerors about 48 A.D.

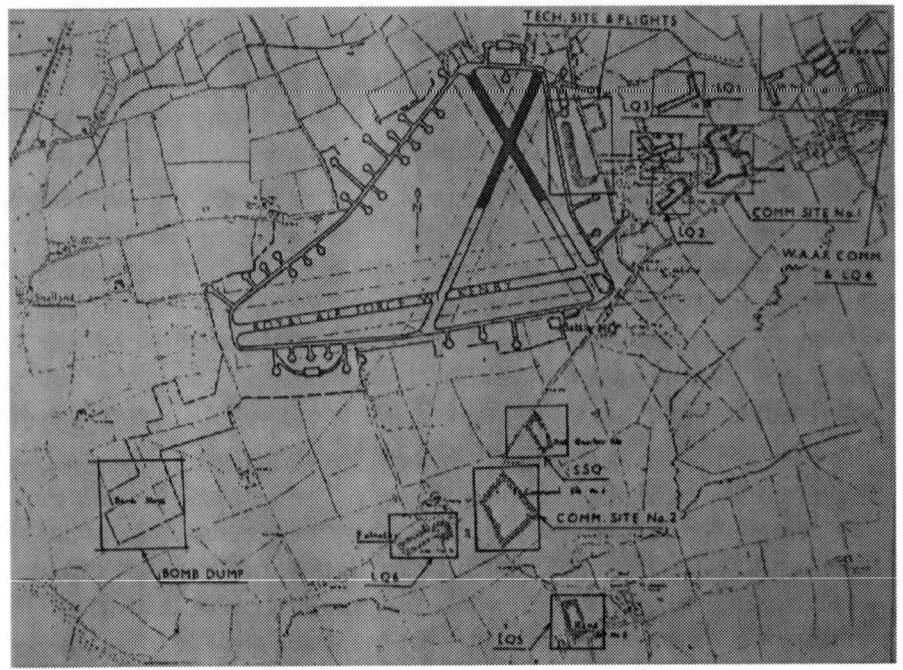

Layout of Wickenby Airfield

Photograph of exhibit in the RAF Wickenby Memorial Museum, May 2005, showing the aerodrome plan

Chapter 5

Our arrival on the squadron was by no means an earth-shattering event. We were dumped unceremoniously on the sacred ground of an operational squadron on July 1st but, even though most of us were Canadians, the date did not seem to be significant. In fact, I don't think any of us gave it a thought.

We gazed at a flat, somewhat pastoral setting interrupted here and there by some nondescript Nissen-type buildings. Twelve Squadron was not located on a permanent station with substantial brick and concrete structures. Instead, this base, as were so many others, was designed for temporary wartime use and the unpainted Nissen huts looked the part.

Jim and I as officers reported to the adjutant and were introduced to the senior squadron officer, a pleasant New Zealand wing commander who welcomed us with a few words. The rest of the crew reported to the station warrant officer

We were assigned quarters in a couple of huts. Jim and I found two empty beds in a long, draughty uncrowded Nissen. We received a cordial greeting from one of our hut-mates, Flight Lieutenant Gray, and settled in. We didn't ask anyone what had happened to our beds' former occupants.

I imagine as we all lay abed that night each mind was filled with thoughts about what the future would bring. Our feelings must have been much the same as those of a sailor about to embark on his first North Atlantic convoy or a soldier who would hear his first shot fired in anger on the morrow. The uncertainty was the worst part.

We knew we were trained well to do our jobs under the ordinary conditions of a cross-country exercise. But what we would be facing would be no exercise. It would be the real thing complete with bombs in the fuselage, anti-aircraft guns on the ground below and possibly Messerschmitts, Focke Wulfes or Junkers 88s in the sky above.

Like others heading into battle for the first time we had no real concept of what it would be like. I am sure each of us wondered how we would face the realities of war and hoped we had not been short changed when courage was handed out.

We knew we would be completely on our own with no one to say, "Do this, do that". Unlike our American allies on heavy bombers, each Lancaster and its crew was a separate and lonely entity whether on night or daylight operations. The U.S. 8th Air Force operated solely by day and flew in massive formations, their silver Vs sparkling in the sunlight. Although their formations were devised to give each aircraft maximum protection against enemy fighters, the Germans managed to exact a heavy toll but often at great cost.

The American saturation bombing technique was totally different from ours. The bombers remained in formation while over the target and their loads were dropped upon a signal from lead bombardiers. We bombed as we flew, individually. Our aircraft formed a loose stream known as a gaggle which, in daylight, made us appear to be strung out all over the sky. But there was method in our apparently disorganized ranks.

We flew according to our orders and were expected to be over target at plus or minus one-half minute of our H-hour. We bombed target indicator flares dropped by our Pathfinder Force aircraft under the direction of a Master Bomber. After dropping our bomb load we flew prescribed courses back to base. In order to work successfully, the operation required precision flying and navigating on the part of the individual crews.

We had only been on the squadron overnight when I discovered that I would be making my first trip over enemy territory that day. This was a familiarization flight that all new pilots were required to take and which was referred to as a "second dickie", the term meaning second pilot.

I was lucky both with the crew I would fly with, an experienced group skippered by my acquaintance of the previous day Flight Lieutenant Gray, and the target which was an easy one. We were to bomb Donleger in France, only a three-hour flight there and back. I discovered that as a "second dickie" I was relegated to the role of observer but, of course, would have been prepared to take over if anything happened to the pilot. Carrying "second dickies" (we took one on two separate occasions) was the only time a trained second pilot was carried in a Lancaster. The rest of the time, Ron, our flight engineer, assisted me during takeoff and landing, handling the controls for flaps and undercarriage and the first throttle setting for takeoff. Although not essential, it was very helpful to have two more hands at these times.

I really don't remember much about my trip with F/L Gray. I know I was impressed with the disciplined, no-nonsense exchanges over the intercom between Gray and the members of his crew as we approached the target. I could not see very well from my seat behind the pilot and engineer but had my first look at the black puffs of flak festooning the sky in the target area. It was over very quickly and we were back on the ground a little more than an hour later. My crew seemed to be happy to see me back in one piece but no happier than I was at my safe return.

After my "second dickie" trip, we spent the next couple of days on flying training including a long six-hour night cross-country exercise.

Then, on July 6, the fateful day arrived! Our crew was on the list for an operation that day. Finally, after the many months of school we were about to take the final exam. This was what our training was all about, not just another cross-country training flight, but a real look at war!

Our bomb-bay would be packed with a load of high explosive devastation destined for an enemy installation. Our gunners would have great belts of live .303 ammunition ready to unleash if the occasion arose. Our navigator, bomb aimer, wireless operator and engineer would be issued with the necessary information to ensure our success. And me, I simply had to do my first ever takeoff with a bomb load and steer the big bird along the right courses and at the right speed, and, of course, make the final decisions.

We filed into the briefing but and immediately discovered the focus of all eyes, the huge map of the British Isles and Europe at the far end of the room -- and the red ribbon that stretched from Wickenby to whatever part of the continent we had been assigned. Ah, that red ribbon, that foreteller of what we faced! That innocent-appearing piece of coloured fabric which could herald a short, relatively easy flip across the Channel into France and back out again. Or a dreaded long voyage through the dark skies over Nazi Germany.

We sighted on that map and ribbon each of the 32 times we stepped through the briefing room doorway. And each time our first view stirred a quiet sigh of relief or a gut-wrench deep within which was never allowed to surface beyond a muttered, "Oh, oh".

On that day, and often afterwards, I thought how unbelievable it was that we, a group of kids (with the exception of our venerable navigator) were involved in this almost dream-like and sometimes nightmarish activity. When we should have been going to school or working at a first job, driving the family car around when we could get it, taking girls to dances and parties, swimming or playing ball, skating or skiing, we were instead flying through alien skies preparing to wreak havoc. We'd been provided with a half-million dollar aircraft, equipped with real 1200-rounds-a-minute machine guns, loaded down with a cargo of high explosives and sent off into the wild blue yonder. *Per Ardua Ad Astra* was the motto of the Royal Air Force -- Through Adversity To The Stars.

All young fellows craved some excitement and adventure. We were being given the chance to fulfill that desire but the odds for survival were not all that inviting. Perhaps this great adventure might prove to be more exciting than we had bargained for in those far-off romantic days of enlistment. But, like marriage, we were firmly caught up in it now for better or worse and the final ending of the drama we were enacting had not yet been written.

These may sound like sombre thoughts but I must admit that my general outlook, and I think this applied to all of us, was one of optimism. We knew we had a duty to perform, that we would give it our best and that we would also strive very hard to survive.

Our first briefing. A crowded, smoky room chock full of aircrew types, most in dull RAF blue battledress, interspersed with the royal blue of the down-under boys. Crews sitting together in a row, a couple of new ones like ourselves quietly awaiting with stoic calm the orders which would send us aloft to face the unknown. Veteran crews lounging with careless abandon chatting, joking and laughing in familiar surroundings.

And all the time the big map loomed, its red route markers unveiled and blatantly summoning us from our playtime to the world of war.

Fortunately the summons did not appear too drastic to our eyes. The ribbon appeared to extend a short distance into occupied France before doubling back in the direction of home. An easy one for starters? We fervently hoped so and while we thus mused about our first op the room was called to attention and the C.O. strode in.

He had a few words of introduction to the day's work, then turned proceedings over to several other officers. "You've got a short, easy one today boys," the intelligence officer intoned, telling us we would be flying to Foret Ducroc in France.

The meteorological officer soothed us with news of good weather; the bombing leader told us what our load would be; the navigation leader described the route. We were given takeoff times, the time to set course, the time to arrive at the target, the height for the bombing run. The aircraft to which we were assigned was already indicated on the list of crews flying the op.

After we broke off Arnold still had a lot of preparations to make as did Jim and Ron. Cal and Jonesy would meet with the gunnery leader for a final word. Arnold would arrive at the aircraft loaded down with maps, charts, a preliminary chart with our course marked, a great deal of data, paper and pencils. He would be a busy man during the flight keeping a running log, plotting our courses and times on his chart and keeping me informed as to course changes etc.

Jim would bring clipboard and information sheets. Ron would also carry a clipboard containing a wealth of forms. Chappy would have his bag of tricks connected with our signals system.

These four were the ones who were really clued in for our trip. My job was to get us there and back, no forms to fill in or calculations to make, thank goodness! The gunners' jobs were also straightforward ones which didn't require any preliminary paper work.

Eventually we were dressed for the occasion and were trucked out to Lancaster J-Jig. The assigned aircraft was of no significance. We simply hoped it was in good shape and able to carry us and our load of destruction to Foret Ducroc and then bring us back to Wickenby with no problems.

Start-up time was signalled by green flares from the control tower. We went through the familiar routine and trundled out along the perimeter track to the runway in use. No radio communication was allowed so the listening enemy would not be tipped off. In fact no phone calls were allowed from the base once an operation was announced.

Then it was our turn to swing onto the long runway and take off.

This takeoff would be different from any I had ever made. In addition to petrol, we were carrying a 15,000-pound load of high explosive bombs -- 15 one thousand pounders. I had no idea how the aircraft would respond to this weighty cargo but knew that Lancs did it all the time so was not particularly worried. However, it was then and there that Ron and I devised our takeoff technique. I set full brakes while he advanced the two inner throttles to the gate. With brakes released the Lanc surged forward and I worked the two outer throttles carefully ahead which gave me steering capability until the tail would lift and the rudders could take over.

It worked fine that time and on all subsequent occasions. We stormed off down the runway, the speed gradually increased, the tail came up and we finally shook ourselves free of the asphalt and kept the nose down to gain precious speed. An aircraft is never more vulnerable than when close to the ground and with a low speed registered on the dial. After a slow and cautious climb away we breathed more easily and began the time-consuming routine to reach assigned height before setting course for France.

Turning onto the prescribed heading we joined a long, strung-out gaggle of other Lancasters heading for France and our target Foret Ducroc. Although I remember many details from subsequent trips, this first operation by our crew has faded into obscurity in my mind. Obviously nothing momentous happened other than the sheer drama of being on our own over enemy territory for the very first time and carrying out the duties for which our long training had prepared us.

I suppose we wondered if we would be attacked by enemy fighters and whether we would be hit by flak. At least we had a look at the flak but not at the fighters. And I suppose we were pleased to return to base unscathed and with one notch on our gun.

Probably the run to Foret Ducroc was anti-climactic, being psyched up to press on come hell or high water, and to end up on a milk run. However, anti-climax or not, we thankfully accepted the ease of accomplishment of Operation No. 1 while being quite well aware that they wouldn't all be "pieces of cake".

BOMBER CREW

Arnold Cowan, navigator

Cal Dagg, rear gunner

JACK E. THOMPSON

CHAPTER 6

On the first page of my Pilot's Flying Log Book, in the section devoted to our days on 12 Squadron, Wickenby, is the notation: "July 18, Lancaster E-Easy PB201, ops Caen S.E." and in the numbers column "4:00 hours".

This terse note disguises in its brevity one of the greatest air operations of World War II.

The Lancasters and Halifaxes took off that July 18, 1944 morning from 'dromes in Yorkshire, Lincolnshire and numerous points south of these counties. They formed into their gaggles and these joined together until the sky was filled with a seemingly never-ending parade of four-engined bombers. Like migrating hawks, although their underparts were black, they streamed southwards and the mighty roar of their passing was heard by all who dwelled or worked far below

The Land Army girls in the fields, the village postmen on their rounds, the factory workers heading for the job or returning from the night shift, housewives in their gardens, children playing -- all heard the thunder of the mighty armada and gazed upwards in awe. The Britishers were used to the sound of aircraft both friendly and hostile. But never before had a sound of such magnitude and a sight of such awesome proportions greeted their ears and eyes. Certainly not one which heralded such a major blow against the enemy.

The people who watched from their towns, villages and farms must have felt a great surge of pride and satisfaction as the bomber force continued to pour southward, heading they knew not where, but undoubtedly bound on a path of destruction against a foe which had shown no mercy. No doubt in many minds echoed the thought, "Old Jerry's going to get it today!"

They were able to read all about it in the next day's papers. The massive raids were hailed as "the greatest air operation in history" and we played a part. In fact, the bombing of Caen was the second trip of our tour.

I had mentioned earlier that we had been disappointed at missing D-Day and the great invasion by our troops of coastal points in occupied France. The trip to Caen was the next best thing because we were taking part in an operation to help our ground forces to push ahead on the victory march.

Allied troops had been stalled outside Caen for some time following their initial successes. This town was heavily fortified and the enemy had put up a stubborn and tenacious defense. Our high command decided it was time for a bomber force to break those defences and allow the armies to move ahead and sweep through France.

In all, 1,000 RAF heavy bombers, Lancasters and Halifaxes, 600 U.S. Liberators and 500 medium bombers and hundreds of light bombers dropped 7,000 tons of high explosives on the German divisions facing our troops that morning. Significantly, the RAF "heavies" alone dropped 5,000 tons.

In a few hours British and Canadian troops, led by the famed General Bernard Montgomery, broke through the shattered German defences.

For us, taking part in this gigantic display of air power was awesome and terribly exciting. To look ahead through the wind-screen and to see a sky full of bombers for as far as our vision extended was drama of the highest sort. Cal's view from the rear turret was equally impressive. He called over the intercom that the sky was crowded with Lancs.

Long before we arrived at Caen we could see the terribly heavy concentrations of flak we would have to fly through. But even this sky full of black puffs couldn't lessen our determination to add our 15,000 pounds to the tons of high explosives wreaking havoc far below. I'm sure the view from ground level of the multitude of aircraft high above coupled with the terrible destruction as the 1,000-pounders exploded, struck terror into the hearts of those enemy troops on the receiving end. I'm sure they must have wondered if the hellish nightmare would ever stop as the Lancs and Hallies droned steadily above in what must have seemed like an endless procession.

On our way to Caen we had met returning formations of U.S. Liberators, their silver bodies and wings glittering in the sunlight. We seemed to meet and pass with awesome swiftness and, of course, our relative speeds were over 400 MPH These aircraft had been attacking targets at St. Lo, another enemy strong-point.

Newspaper accounts helped us to understand what had taken place at Caen. This is a quotation from one such story:

> A foremost target was the steel works at Mondeville, in the eastern suburbs of Caen, which the Germans had turned into an extremely powerful strong-point.
>
> It had numbers of mortars which kept up a continuous five against our troops. Here, also, the enemy had strongly fortified himself with anti-tank and anti-aircraft guns.
>
> Great numbers of enemy troops, too, were reported to be in position there.
>
> The Mondeville steel works and another enemy strong-point at Colombelles ... were alone attacked by more than 500 Lancasters and Halifaxes.

RAF Spitfires provided the escort for the U.S. Liberators, which bombed nearby St. Lo, since 750 American heavy bombers were attacking targets in Germany at the same time as the Caen and St. Lo operation. This kept American fighter escorts busy.

According to a newspaper story, "The Spitfire pilots had a grandstand view of the great attack and, in their view, the German army has never been subjected to such a grim morning."

To have been a part of such a giant operation which destroyed a major stumbling block for our ground forces was pretty inspiring for a very new, very green crew. We knew that at Caen we had helped to bring the end of the war a little closer. None of our other 30 operations were a patch on this one for the tremendous pride we felt in having been there. So we missed D-Day, so what? A U.S. colonel who flew that day was quoted as saying, "This operation had D-Day beat by a mile!"

No enemy fighters came to the defense of Caen. The newspaper account states, "One very significant outcome of these attacks is that the Germans employed their massed flak batteries to the utmost possible extent, but, apart from causing battle damage to numbers of aircraft, they proved a pitiful substitute for fighter opposition."

The huge bombing operation was completed in three hours for the loss of only nine aircraft from among the more than 2100 involved.

Photograph from G - George during raid on Le Havre

CHAPTER 7

The Lancaster bombers we flew were designed for one purpose, to transport up to 15,000 pounds of destruction to a prescribed location and to unleash the awesome load of devastating explosives with accuracy. Far removed from the earth-bound scene being drenched with a rain of hurtling missiles, we gave little thought to the lives below us and concentrated mainly on the precision of our work and our own safety. We took pride in being part of a great battle which was slowly and surely bringing us closer to victory over a foe sworn to destroy and enslave the people of our world.

Each time we filed into the locker room and started dressing for a flight, picking up our parachutes and other paraphernalia and making our laden way to the waiting truck, I'm sure all of us felt we were heading into the unknown. In spite of all the trips as the tour continued this was a feeling that never could be surmounted; we could never become blasé and shrug off the possibility of not returning despite an increasing familiarity with operations.

A favourite superstition handed down to new squadron members was that the first five and last five trips in the tour were the ones when most crews disappeared. This seemed to be borne out on many occasions.

I remember one pilot in particular, an older, more mature RAF type who looked extremely competent. He was a tall, swarthy handsome man, obviously with a bit of money, because he drove an MG while almost all on the squadron rode bicycles or walked. He and his crew were veterans with many ops to their credit. It was a shock to learn that his aircraft failed to return one night. So you never knew what the next trip over the continent held in store for you, veterans or not!

The ultimate commitment to face whatever lay in store for us came as we clambered one by one up the little ladder which led to the side door and into the big machine. Here the utility of the aircraft became apparent. Unpainted metal sides and roof of the fuselage and two heavy, bare spars which had to be climbed over, greeted our eyes as we made our way to our widespread positions. The deadly load we carried in the 30-foot bomb bay was hidden by flooring containing inspection panels.

There was a lot of room in a Lancaster fuselage. Thirty or forty bodies could have been accommodated, very uncomfortably, but nevertheless packed into that 70-foot long fuselage. For the seven of us it was very roomy and yet most of the positions were relatively cramped.

Jim's quarters in the nose were quite spacious. He had enough room to lie prone, his eye glued to the bomb-sight or to stand in the forward gun turret which housed two Browning .303s. There was also space to stack great quantities of "window". These were bundles of foil strips he was required to release from the aircraft through a small opening at prescribed intervals.

"Window" was the code designation for the thousands of strips dropped from aircraft which danced and pirouetted through the sky and were supposed to confuse the very devil out of enemy radar which was attempting to home in on individual aircraft. Jim religiously popped the bundles down the chute and we all hoped that his efforts and those of other bomb aimers were having the desired effect.

The nose section where Jim lived during our trips was several steps below the level of the main floor. Behind the nose, in the next section was the cockpit where Ron and I held forth. My seat was on the left side and had armour plating on its back and a couple of folding arms which made the whole thing the most comfortable position in the plane. Ron, on the other hand, who sat beside me, had to make do with a little folding seat which must have been uncomfortable as the hours droned by.

Before our eyes was a bank of instruments which extended across the width of the cockpit below the windscreen. In front of me were all the flight instruments -- air speed indicator, needle and ball, rate of climb and descent, gyro, artificial horizon, DR compass and standard compass. Ron looked directly at all the engine instruments, four of each since there were four engines. These included oil temperature and pressure, cylinder head temperature, manifold pressure, RPM indicator, boost gauges and so on. This great array of dials was a far cry from the needle, ball and airspeed plus a couple of engine gauges that I had started out with at Elementary Flying School in Canada. But by this time we were conversant with the assortment and could see at a glance if anything was wrong either with flying or engine performance.

One thing which puzzled me for some time was the way Ron would stare out the window on his side, then look past me out the window on my side. I looked out the alternate windows myself but all I could see were our wings and engines sitting there in their normal positions, nothing unusual, nothing different. I finally, one day, asked him what he was looking at and he told me he was synchronizing the engines. As far as I knew the engines were synchronized when all four RPM gauges registered the same but that just shows how much I needed an engineer. He pointed out that a whirling pattern could be seen between the two sets of propellers on either side. By minute adjustments of the two RPM levers for one pair of motors this whirling pattern came to a standstill and *voila!*, the motors were synchronized.

I never did find out whether perfect synchronization contributed to the aircraft's performance or whether it was a matter of engineering pride to achieve this ultimate adjustment. But Ron was a perfectionist and we were sure in sync!

Passing along from the cockpit towards the tail, the first little cramped compartment was occupied by our wise-cracking wireless operator. Chappy had a desk, a wireless key for transmissions and a receiver. If he wanted to take a peek outside he could stand up and peer out the astrodome, a half-round "skylight" projecting above the fuselage. This was provided in case the navigator decided to get down to some real old-fashioned navigation and take star shots with a sextant.

Arnold, our navigator, had a tiny office and was completely cut off from any view of the outside world on night trips because his blackout curtain had to be closed to prevent any light from escaping. Arnold claims that he kept tucked away in his little private cubby hole and never did look out, especially over the target, but I doubt if this was true. I think natural curiosity would force him to take a peek from time to time just to prove to himself what it was we were really doing.

If one were to move back along the fuselage from Arnold's position a pair of legs would be seen projecting downwards from the roof. The rest of the body was enclosed in a Plexiglas dome which protruded above the fuselage. Called the mid-upper turret, this is where Jonesy held forth with his twin .303 Brownings. Jonesy could rotate his turret 360 degrees so he could fire in any direction and, of course had the best view of any of us. Fortunately an interrupter was built into the system which prevented him from shearing off pieces of our twin fins and rudders which extended well above the top of the aircraft.

"Tail-end Charlie" was the apt description applied to those who rode forth to do battle from the rear turret. Our "Charlie", Cal, had the loneliest position imaginable. Suspended in space behind the tail plane, Cal was squeezed into a part-plexiglass bubble with only enough space for the butt ends of his four .303 Brownings. The rear of the turret through which the gun barrels projected was wide open to the outside world. If it hadn't been for his electrically heated suit Cal would probably have frozen to death on a cold night. At 20,000 feet the temperature would have been 40 degrees lower than at ground level. The rear turret could be rotated 180 degrees and the guns could be elevated and depressed to cover a fair amount of sky. Cal had the distinction of being the only one aboard who saw only where we had been rather than where we were going.

A letter from Cal written in response to a request for information gave some idea of what it was really like away back there. Cal wrote:

> I had a few fears on ops, but then, I suppose we all did. Mine was being all alone so far away in the tail. I was always afraid of being wounded and being on my own and having to patch myself up. Or being trapped in the aircraft if we were shot down and I was unable to get out. The rear turret scared me at first; you could not see the rest of the aircraft, only the fins and rudders. It was like being on the end of a pole -- and the turret was a hard thing to get out of. The firing of the four-gun turret was terrific. I actually got a big kick out of all that firepower. The noise was hard on the ears from four guns and the recoil being so close to my body was scary but I got used to that.

Cal didn't mention that the rear turret was also the most vulnerable position in the aircraft. If an enemy fighter could knock out the rear gunner he could easily close in for a total kill from below and behind a Lancaster with no fear of being hit.

My hat is off to Cal and all other rear gunners who lived dangerously and who often died alone.

We had a number of preparations to make as we flew towards continental Europe. One of the most important was checking the oxygen system to make sure all seven of us were receiving that life-sustaining flow. It was the rule that oxygen masks were put on at 10,000 feet and were worn constantly until that level was reached on the return flight.

The masks became uncomfortable after several hours but a little discomfort was a small price to pay for keeping us alive. Pressurization as provided in modern passenger aircraft was, of course, unknown and would likely have proved impractical with the great possibility of the fuselage being holed by enemy fire.

Having the mask on was also handy because our intercom mikes were then in position and there was no need to fumble around in the case of a sudden emergency call. When the masks were left hanging by one strap from our helmets it seemed that someone always left a microphone switched on and had to be reminded in no uncertain terms that the noise of the aircraft rumbling through the head-phones didn't make for pleasant listening.

When we arrived over the increasingly familiar English Channel, the gunners' monotonously lonely vigils were momentarily interrupted as they tested their Brownings. The combination of their six .303s being fired vibrated throughout the aircraft and the smell of cordite wafted along the fuselage. It was vitally important that the guns be checked out to make certain that no stoppages or other malfunctions would prevent their firing should defense against an enemy fighter suddenly be required.

Chappy in the meantime was on the alert listening through his headphones for any wireless transmissions. During the flight he would receive messages which updated the winds that he would pass on to Arnold. On the homeward trip he would hear reports on the weather at base and, in the unlikely event of a diversion to another airport, would alert the pilot and navigator.

On a couple of occasions our aircraft was designated to send back an updated wind or a "duty carried out" message to base after our bomb load was dropped. We were never very keen on this duty because we knew a transmission could be picked up almost instantly which could be used to 'home" a fighter on our position. I know that Chappy keyed a very fast message each time lasting not more than 15 seconds and we hoped this would prevent disclosing our position.

I'm afraid we didn't give much thought to the tremendous preparation and the numbers of people involved in sending us winging off on another operation. Bomber Command headquarters would initiate the whole thing. Crews had a favourite story that Air Chief Marshall Arthur (Bomber) Harris used to stand with his eyes closed in front of the map of Europe and toss a dart in order to pick the next target.

In any case, the planning was carried out at the top and the orders filtered down through group and wing and finally to the squadron. Weather reports were received and routes worked out. I don't think we ever flew directly to a German target. We changed course several times before settling on the bearing which would lead us to our real destination. This, of course, was done to confuse the enemy and thwart the movement of fighters to a certain area until it was too late.

In addition to the route changes, diversions by a few bombers were often scheduled so that German defences could not be sure which general area would come under attack.

As well as the route, the bombing attack which usually included several hundred aircraft, had to be coordinated. Obviously chaos would result from the arrival of the whole force at the same time in the air space above the target. Even heights had to be varied to prevent too great a concentration and also to confuse the anti-aircraft gunners. We were always pleased if we were assigned to one of the greater heights, not nearly as happy about a lower altitude designation. For one thing it was definitely preferable to run less risk of being hit by the discharged bombs from a higher flying air-craft. For another, we felt safer from accurate anti-aircraft fire the further we were above the ground.

At our own base, as at the other bomber squadrons, receipt of an operational order resulted in a sudden great flurry of activity.

Often there were only a few hours in which to prepare. But the ground crews were efficient and ready to cope. Engines had to be run up and the aircraft checked over thoroughly inside and out. Great quantities of window usually had to be packed in the nose compartment. The all-important cargo, the reason for the whole exercise, had to be carefully ferried via tractor-drawn trains of low-slung dollies to each Lancaster. Here the bombs were hand-loaded with chain-hoists into their racks. Since they were filled with high explosives and very heavy, handling this great load of destruction required expertise and the utmost care. While the aircraft were undergoing all this attention another crew was busy with petrol bowsers topping up the capacious fuel tanks.

Sometimes, it was possible to get a little advance knowledge about the trip in store for us by learning from ground crew about the fuel and bomb loads. If they told us it was a "cookie" and incendiaries we knew we were in for a long one. Although the cylindrical canister of high explosive which was the "cookie" weighed 4,000 pounds, the load of incendiaries was relatively light, the combination allowing us to carry a lot of petrol.

In contrast was a bomb bay filled with 15 one-thousand-pound high explosive bombs. With 15,000 pounds to carry, the fuel load had to be considerably less and, therefore, the trip much shorter.

Of course, learning that a long trip was scheduled heightened the anxiety until briefing time when the target was identified. I always wanted to go once to that most famous of targets, Berlin, about which Hermann Goering, the Luftwaffe head, had once boasted, "No bomb will fall on Berlin". This was during the early days of World War II when the Luftwaffe was raining bombs on London and other English cities and its swarms of fighters were prepared to defend the German capital against retaliation. Of course Fat Hermann's empty boast was soon refuted by the RAF which continued to hit Berlin during all the war years.

It would have been a significant entry to have in our log books, but at the same time, an infinitely safer tour would result from avoiding that heavily defended capital of Nazidom. However, we were never called upon to press our luck with a Berlin foray.

Original Wickenby Control Tower(above). The hazy view of the Lincoln Cathedral from Wickenby airfield. Both photos May 2005.

CHAPTER 8

We discovered on our first night trip that things were literally as different as day and night. Some aspects were better, some much worse.

We were wrapped in such a cloak of darkness that we felt absolutely alone even though we knew that we were accompanied by dozens of RAF heavy bombers. Our first night trip was to Courtrai in Belgium and we'd been told by the intelligence officer during briefing that we could expect a fair number of German night fighters in the area. This, of course, held true for most of our subsequent night trips, usually into Germany. But the officer's warning immediately conjured up images of tracer-directed machine gun and cannon onslaughts slicing through our aircraft and our flesh. It was not a comforting reminder to carry with us on our way to Courtrai.

The Belgian target was a short trip, only three hours, but our inexperience made it seem like a never-ending run through a black void bristling with an enemy determined to shoot us down.

The operation started normally as we followed the dim perimeter lights and taxied out for take-off. Already I had learned one thing about squadron take-offs. The aircraft next in line was given the green light to go before the one in front had cleared the runway. Sometimes, if one eagerly slammed on the power and lifted off it would be to find one's aircraft violently buffeted by the slipstream of the Lancaster ahead. Because of this highly uncomfortable performance while one was barely off the ground with a heavy bomb load and struggling to build up flying speed, I always hesitated, sometimes receiving two or three more greens before opening the throttles. No doubt this was slightly disruptive to an efficient squadron launch, but I'm sure our few seconds' delay did not reflect on the war effort or even the squadron effort. It did keep us in one piece.

We climbed away and headed for the nearby east coast. We would turn at the coast and fly back again gaining as much height as possible while waiting for our time to set course for Courtrai. During this period we had some reassuring chatter over the intercom which later would remain relatively silent as all concentrated on the job at hand.

Jim, from the nose, eventually reported that he could see the south coast and then later that we were passing near Dunkirk on the French side of the Channel. An ack-ack battery at Dunkirk opened up and we later discovered this greeting from the enemy occupying this coastal town was standard procedure whenever we flew by. Probably manning their anti-aircraft guns at Dunkirk was a very boring and generally unnoted duty made only bearable by a chance to fire away at the high flyers overhead. We didn't worry about this show of strength and wished that all the defences we would encounter would be as ineffective.

Now we were flying over Continental Europe and nerves suddenly became taut. The black night was a friend, but, at the same time, a foe. Our aircraft was as invisible as we could make it. The wing-tip and tail navigation lights had been doused before we left friendly airspace. The instrument panel in the cockpit glowed with green phosphorescence but otherwise Ron and I sat in total darkness. Arnold's light was on in his compartment but his blackout curtain prevented any tell-tale gleams from escaping.

One thing we couldn't do anything about was the cold, blue flicker from our engine exhausts. To me the exhaust flames seemed very bright and a dead give-away but I imagine they were not as visible as I feared.

A sudden drop of the port wing which I immediately flipped up again, the abrupt motion transferred to the starboard wing -- then smooth air once more. What was that? Then I realized we had hit the slipstream of another Lanc or Halifax flying a short distance ahead. This happened frequently on night trips momentarily startling us and then reassuring us that we were probably on track and also not alone in the forbidding, enemy-haunted blackness. No matter how often we sashayed about, caught in a slipstream, I was always startled by its suddenness and violence and really found small comfort in the knowledge that a friend was on track. I knew we would be, given Arnold's superb navigation.

After we had reached Courtrai and dropped our bombs we continued to fly in a southerly direction for several minutes until Arnold, sounding flustered, called up on the intercoms, "Tommy, we're over Lille. Alter course to 340 right now! Get the hell out of here!" Arnold had forgotten to give me a course change coming out of the target and we were bang in the middle of a heavily defended area.

I banked sharply and cracked on some more throttle and we got the hell out of there. In spite of the fact that the Belgian city was shown on the map as bristling with anti-aircraft defences, not one gun opened fire and we began to breathe more easily in a couple of minutes. Perhaps the gun crews on duty couldn't be bothered to fire at a lone pigeon trespassing in their air space.

Just a couple of nights after our night-operation baptism we were briefed for a trip to Kiel near the base of the peninsula which juts north from Germany into Denmark. A big German naval base, Kiel was an important target for our bombs.

It was a long haul across the North Sea and we were ordered to fly below 1,000 feet to try to evade enemy radar for as long as possible. At a certain point we had to begin our climb to operational height. With the cold, wind-tossed sea not far below and a total cloud overcast just 1,000 feet above, it felt as though we were making our way through a vast never-ending tunnel although it was difficult to see either water or cloud on this dark night. But we knew they were there and it didn't do for a pilot to let his attention wander from the instruments. Although not threatening in any way, that low cloud base had a somewhat claustrophobic effect but we would be more than pleased to find the haven the heavy stratus layers would provide on the way home.

We eventually made our climb up through the cloud, emerging into a clear night sky. And then, many minutes before we arrived at the target area, we sighted its brilliance erupting into the darkness ahead.

"Come on in boys, the flak's not bad," a cool British voice crackled through our headphones. This was the Master Bomber flying a Lanc or Mosquito and giving the Pathfinder crews their directions where to drop their indicator flares. He would remain over the target area at a low altitude throughout the raid, beset from above by the chance of being hit by falling bombs, from below by the huge barrage the ack-ack gunners were hurling skywards.

This was our first look at a major target under attack by night. It was an awe-inspiring phantasm of light, the bright orange of flame, the sparkling diamonds of incendiaries, the red and green target indicators dropped by Pathfinders, the bright, white probing fingers of searchlights, the thousands of crackling glitters of anti-aircraft fire. And silhouetted against the brilliance below, the countless dark puffs of expended ack-ack shells and the plumes of rising dark smoke from ground-level fires and explosions.

As we droned over Kiel, we had a ringside seat from which to marvel at the great destructive forces unleashed against the enemy. While fascinated by a sight we would witness many more times, we were also very much aware of our vulnerability, the three or four minutes we spent on the bombing run seeming like an eternity.

We were briefed to make our bomb run at 160 MPH which seemed like a slow crawl through a highly dangerous piece of sky. Not only did it seem deadly slow but the very fact that we had to fly straight and level for several minutes contributed to our anxiety. But it couldn't be any other way. There was no point in making the long trip and then messing up the whole purpose of the exercise by a careless run-up to the aiming point.

We chugged along with bomb doors open and waited impatiently as Jim told me, "Left, left steady; right steady; steady, steady, steady." And then the triumphant shout of "Bombs away," the lurch upward of the aircraft suddenly tons lighter. The bomb doors closing, nose down slightly, throttles ahead and we were driving into the welcoming shroud of the surrounding darkness, the adrenalin surges lessening as we left that glimpse of hell behind and set course for home. But the adrenalin was scheduled to be unleashed into our systems once again before the trip was over.

We were banking onto a course change when the blackness ahead and to starboard was suddenly interrupted by a bright path of tracers which seemed to float lazily towards us. We were being fired upon by an aircraft until then invisible in the darkness. It turned out to be another Lanc whose tail gunner probably thought we were a fighter on a curve of pursuit. We tightened our bank and got out of there having a laugh over this case of mistaken identity.

But we weren't laughing a few minutes later when the gunners informed us that we had company, a German Junkers 88 night fighter. Cal and Jonesy started firing away at the aircraft which was starboard of our stern in a good position to make an attack.

I could have started us into a corkscrew but I didn't. Instead I shoved the control column ahead and we nosed into a fairly steep dive heading for the clouds several thousand feet below. I didn't pay too much attention to the air speed but I'm almost certain we exceeded the maximum allowable speed of 360 MPH before we disappeared into the comforting embrace of the ten-tenths cloud.

Then it was time to slow down and level out. I did not want to do this too abruptly possibly applying a fatal strain to the wings, and aside from that, I found that pulling out was not an easy task. There was a lot of tension on the control column. With the throttles back and with the help of the elevator trim tabs, we gradually levelled out and resumed our normal 220 MPH cruising speed.

Every once in a while as we flew toward England, we popped up to the top of the cloud cover for a look around much like a groundhog sticking its nose out of its hole. We thought perhaps the German fighter could follow us using radar. A quick look around, then down we went again. Whether it was imagination or not, our gunners thought they spotted him in the blackness so we kept to the comforting canopy for many miles until we decided he had given up the chase.

Wouldn't you know that this was the only trip we made that the navigation section decided to plot all of our positions at a certain point on the return journey. At the next briefing they projected a slide on the screen showing all aircraft on track except for good old J-Jig that was miles off course. In all the excitement, Arnold had forgotten to allow for our great change in speed and so had missed a course alteration at a certain time. It didn't matter as he soon discovered the error and made a correction.

However, the rest of the crews had a good laugh when they saw that slide until it was mentioned that we had encountered a Junkers 88 fully intent to shoot us down.

Allerton Hall, 6 Group Headquarters, near Knaresborough, North Yorkshire, May 2005

Lincoln Cathedral, 2005

CHAPTER 9

Flying at night over occupied Europe and Germany gave me a strange feeling of almost dream-like quality. Just to be flying through the blackness in a big aeroplane seemed unreal. And even more mind-boggling was the fact that we were on a mission to wreak havoc with our deadly cargo while fighter planes were doing their best to find us and shoot us down.

We were accompanied by many friends on these trips whom we could not see but we knew that, should we get into trouble, the friends would be of no avail. We were strictly on our own as we flew steadily into the unknown with each minute of the flight taking us farther from home.

This very aloneness was demonstrated to us graphically and unforgettably on our first operation to Stuttgart. Jonesy in the mid-upper turret reported that he could see a German Heinkel 111 attacking a Lancaster slightly ahead and to our starboard. The two aircraft were a few hundred feet above us.

Seconds later Jonesy yelled over the intercom, "Dive, Tommy, dive!" which, I did immediately not knowing the reason but also not delaying to ask questions. "He's coming right for us!" was Jonesy's next dramatic message. By this time I could see the flaming Lanc sideslipping through the sky right in our direction. As we continued to lose height the blazing bomber slipped over our heads and continued earthwards in a long ,spiral dive. We saw no parachutes.

As this nerve-shattering incident happened in the early part of the trip it served as an unpleasant introduction to our Stuttgart flight. We made three trips to that target and hated every one of them. First of all, they were very long, over eight hours each time. During at least six hours of each trip we were subjected to unrelenting nervous tension. By the time we returned to base from one of the Stuttgart runs we were worn to a frazzle.

During the Stuttgart operations we searched the sky like we had never searched before, each of us concentrating on the patch we could see, watching for that tell-tale dark shadow which was not a part of the surrounding blackness. As we approached the target area we knew that we were in fighter-infested air space and we all remembered that flaming Lancaster.

Stuttgart itself was a crazy patchwork of light, a huge surrealist painting of Dante's Inferno. The continuous flashes of exploding bombs mingled with the white-hot incendiary clusters, the rising pall of smoke, the crackling flak bursts, the thousands of black puffs which floated serenely by, the criss-crossing of vapour trails from fighter planes. It was like watching a silent movie photographed in Technicolor because, of course, we couldn't hear any of the sound which accompanied the visual effects.

Then away from the holocaust we had helped to create and back along "fighter alley" for the long, tense homeward journey. I think it was Cal's suggestion that I should bank the aircraft in each direction at rapid intervals so the gunners could look below. The belly of the Lanc was completely unprotected and highly vulnerable to an unseen surprise attack. So we charged along dropping the wings alternately while Cal and Jonesy checked the black void below. These manoeuvres were tiring for me because I had to keep us on course at the same time. They must have been very uncomfortable for the rest of the crew but worth every moment of tiredness or discomfort if they served to protect us from being raked by the cannons or machineguns of a fighter.

As it turned out we saw very few of the enemy during these Stuttgart missions. But not all crews were as lucky. Our good friend Frank Watt had a hairy experience with two fighters attempting to attack him at the same time. He was able to give them the slip but had a wild tale to tell in the mess the next day.

I think it was at this time with the experience of a few operations tucked away that we as a crew developed a philosophy of survival. Jonesy claimed in later years that he became a fatalist -- if it was going to happen, it was going to happen. Ron told me very recently at a crew reunion that he felt all along that we were going to have to "walk out", in other words would have to parachute from a damaged aircraft.

I'm not sure about Jim's feelings since he was so superstitious but he seemed to indicate that if we didn't change anything (such as having symbols painted on the aircraft) things should work out.

In spite of these personal thoughts of Jonesy and Ron that we were living on borrowed time, I think we all realized that luck or fate played only a partial role in our continuing survival. That our own actions could contribute greatly to our chances was an accepted fact and thus we operated with the maximum amount of efficiency at all times. This involved, among other things, remaining on course, on prescribed height and time -- and watching, always watching.

Handling our duties in this way also helped us to fulfill another philosophy -- that there was no percentage in risking our necks unless we intended carrying out our operational orders to the best of our ability. Our job was to bomb the enemy, to help destroy his ability to make war. So we flew at our assigned height even though we often wanted to escape the bursting flak by climbing; we kept our bombing run speed at 160 MPH even though we wanted to shove on full throttles and scoot away from the inferno; we maintained straight and level flight to ensure our bomb aimer's accurate release even though every nerve cried out that we were sitting ducks for the anti-aircraft gunners.

On our third trip to Stuttgart, which occurred a couple of months after the first two operations to that target, a new factor was added to the obstacles already present along that lone corridor of nerve-tingling uncertainty. This was the weather which had not been foretold with accuracy by the meteorologists. Surprisingly enough weather generally had little effect on our trips. But this time we encountered towering cumulus and cumulo-nimbus clouds and had to leave our assigned height to climb above the dangerous blockade stretching across our path. These types of clouds were beautiful to behold but no fun to fly through. The awesome force of updrafts and downdrafts within the great mountain peaks of vapour had often spelled doom for an aircraft, ripping it apart and sending its pieces spinning downward.

With this knowledge in mind we began to climb from 18,000 feet. It was a slow ascent in the ratified air three and one-half miles above ground level but we gradually reached and slid over the tops of the threatening giants. It was at 23,000 feet when we were able to level out, the highest any of us had ever been or would ever be again in wartime flying. At that altitude, the Lancaster proved sluggish and slow to respond and we were glad to be able to descend soon to a more normal height.

One incident of particular interest took place on our second Stuttgart sortie. We were stooging along on our way towards a turning point which would lead us to the target. Rear-gunner Cal suddenly yelled over the intercom that we had a Focke Wulfe 190, a famed German fighter, behind us. Then we heard the rapid pounding of Cal's four machine guns coupled with a triumphant announcement, "I got him, I got him". Evidently the FW 190 dove away from Cal's vicious onslaught and our gunner thought he had scored a victory. Unfortunately this was never confirmed officially, a procedure which required sightings logged by the crews of other aircraft.

At any rate Cal had his great moment of excitement and must still wonder whether there was one less FW 190 available to fly another night.

CHAPTER 10

All flying stations had a call sign, a code word which was used by pilots to call up the control tower and receive landing instructions.

Wickenby had probably the most appropriate designation in all of Bomber Command. Our station's call sign was "Grateful" and there is no question that we were more than grateful to catch our first glimpse of the aerodrome after an operation.

But long before our arrival at Wickenby, our return to friendly shores was heralded at night by the sudden appearance of a myriad of tiny red, green and white lights which suddenly blinked on in the blackness like the beacons of fireflies. As we all arrived over England we switched on our navigation lights -- green on the star-board wing, red on the port side and white on the tail. The little lights which appeared in all parts of the sky around us were a reminder that we had not been unaccompanied during our lonely night vigil. They also alerted us to the fact that scores of other big bombers were sharing the air space above a relatively narrow strip of countryside and that we needed to keep a careful watch. All of the hazards were not created by the enemy.

As we neared Lincolnshire, from where many of the bombers originated, we gradually separated as a host of landing fields beckoned their returning warriors. Right around our home station of Wickenby two dozen squadrons of Lancasters would be finding their home bases and beginning the stacked-up circling which preceded landing.

The first sight of Wickenby by night was fairy-like, a sparkling myriad of tiny diamonds shimmering on the dark floor of the earth. As we drew closer the tiny glittering pin-points grew into a circular perimeter of bright lights with the long lance of the runway projecting across the circle. It was at this point that I made my first call to the control tower, no long nattering like we sometimes heard from U.S. Air Force 'dromes, but just a short and sweet "Grateful from George, over."

That was enough to tell the flying control officer that G - George had arrived safely and was awaiting landing instructions. The response in the cool, business-like voice of a WAAF operator was equally short, "George 3,000, over". This message meant to us that we would be required to circle the 'drome at 3,000 feet until further directions were given. So we would make our way around that huge lighted circle counter-clockwise. It was an unvarying rule in the air force that you always made a left-hand circuit which, of course gave the pilot sitting in the left seat the best visibility.

As we continued to orbit we were well aware that the circuit of the nearest bomber aerodrome just about intersected our own. We had to be constantly on the look-out for an aircraft circling the next airfield at the same height whose pilot may have wandered a little too close to our own air space. Collisions and near-collisions were not unknown.

Also on the alert were Jonesy and Cal, maintaining a vigilant watch from their turrets. Enemy fighters had been known to follow a bomber stream home and then cause havoc by shooting down bombers right over their own aerodrome.

With our flight control's usual efficiency we knew it would not be long before we received orders to descend to a lower level and then, finally, to find ourselves on the final approach to the long, brightly-lit runway. The perimeter light circle was our guide to finding the proper landing direction. As we flew the circle, now down to 1,000 feet, we encountered a break in the circular pattern and a lead-in of lights directly to the runway. This was known as the funnel.

By this time, Ron would have popped the undercarriage selector and the green lights on the panel showed the wheels were down and locked. We were unable to see the wheels under the wings, so had to depend on the green indicators. Ron would then dump the flaps and we would settle into the relatively-steep nose-down attitude of final approach.

Of great value to a pilot guiding a big Lancaster towards the parallel lines of lights indicating the edges of the runway was a neat piece of gadgetry called the glide path indicator. This consisted of three coloured lights which told the pilot at the controls whether he was too high, too low or right on. Amber called for less power in order to sink faster, red more power to slow the downward descent and green, sweet perfection. Degrees of over or under shoot were also shown with combinations of green-amber or green-red.

After landing and a slow taxi along the perimeter track to the hardstand where our aircraft was parked, we shut everything down and clambered awkwardly from the Lanc carting parachutes and other assorted items. Our big hope at that point was that transport would come shortly to cart us to the briefing hut we had left hours before. Here we had a thorough interrogation about everything we had seen, or thought we had seen, before we were finally able to bolt a quick meal and hit the sack.

Flight control always did a first-rate job handling the sudden influx of aircraft arriving overhead. They kept things moving in an orderly fashion with Lancs touching down about every two minutes. Occasionally their orderly procedure was interrupted and put on hold when an emergency occurred. One such I remember vividly. A Canadian skipper, F/L Foote, called up and announced that his Lanc was badly shot up and that he had two wounded crewmen aboard. All orbiting aircraft were given orders to keep circling at their assigned heights until further notice.

We happened to have just landed before the emergency call came through so we quickly taxied clear of the runway, then waited to see how Foote managed. I'm sure all crews aloft and everyone else up and about and aware of the situation held their collective breath as the big Lanc came charging in at a higher than normal speed. I believe his hydraulics had been damaged. Under Foote's skilful handling the aircraft landed, then sped down the runway at a frightening pace. I'm not sure whether his brakes were gone but, realizing he wasn't going to get stopped, the pilot applied hard rudder and swung the machine into a sudden, skidding ground-loop which neatly wiped off the undercarriage. The Lanc slid along sideways on its belly for a short distance then came to a stop in a cloud of dust.

For his skilful nursing home of the ailing Lanc and getting his wounded crew members to medical aid as soon as possible, F/L Foote was awarded an immediate DSO (Distinguished Service Order). He was a member of 626 Squadron which shared Wickenby with our own 12 Squadron.

A humorous example of how closely the airfields were situated to each other happened one day when we were returning to Wickenby from a training flight. We circled round the 'drome and I called up "Grateful" and received permission to land. We were swinging into our final cross-wind leg and Ron and I were making our landing check when suddenly somebody who was looking more closely at the ground than either Ron or I called, "That's not Wickenby!"

Sure enough, when we examined the airfield, we realized that we were preparing to land at the wrong one, three or four miles from home. We got out of there in a hurry and hustled into the Wickenby circuit.

My landings were never very consistent as the crew can testify. The Lanc often managed to baffle me by floating beautifully along when I was expecting to touch down. This sometimes resulted in a couple of bounces as I attempted to coax the machine to settle down. One such landing was duly noted by our flight commander who was escorting the visiting Air Officer Commanding our wing. Squadron Leader Corrie told me afterwards, "Here I am in the control tower with the AOC watching the squadron land. When you were coming in I said to him, 'This is one of our most experienced crews landing, sir' and damned if you didn't bounce all the way down the runway!"

JACK E. THOMPSON

Jim Peacock, bomb aimer (left) and Gerald Jones, mid-upper gunner (middle) and Jack Chapman, wireless operator (bottom)

CHAPTER 11

Our flying experiences while on operations were not all grim. In fact we had some very interesting and pleasant times mixed in with the more serious aspects.

Probably the most rewarding part of any flight was when we came in sight of Wickenby, our base, once again. In daylight we could see the magnificent towers of ancient Lincoln Cathedral, high on a hill in the City of Lincoln, just ten miles from Wickenby. The cathedral was a comforting and reassuring landmark, a reminder that we had come home unscathed from another sortie against the enemy.

I still recall with great delight a flight over southern England on a perfect autumn evening when we were on our second trip to Duisburg. The low, late sun threw the villages, towns, neat fields, gardens and hedges into sharp relief, an effect which made everything appear utterly peaceful. We were flying low, just a few hundred feet above the ground, and could see everything in the sharpest detail. The quiet countryside bathed in the warm light of an imminent sunset was such a contrast with what I knew we would be watching from on high over Duisburg within a couple of hours. It was almost enough to make one forget for a moment that we were engaged in more than a sight-seeing joy-ride.

Another time, nearing England after a night trip, I was having a ball skimming over the tops of moon-illuminated cumulus clouds. I would pull the aircraft over a fluffy cloud peak, then dive sharply down the other side into the valley between it and the next one. I was having such a good time that I forgot that the other six guys in the aircraft might not have been enjoying the roller-coaster ride they were getting. But I received a reminder from Jim, riding up in the nose, who suddenly exclaimed over the intercom, "For God's sake, Tommy, cut it out will you!" I quickly settled down, with regret, into our customary sedate, straight and level flight.

Another few minutes of fun that I recall was also experienced on a night return when we flew directly over the great expanse of tidal flats known as The Wash. A deep indentation in the eastern coastline, The Wash was often a reference point for us during our flights east and west as we gained height before setting out on a trip.

This night our course led us over the huge, shallow bay and, since illumination was good, I dropped down close to the surface for a bit of low flying. We swooped down across the waters and flatlands, thrilled (at least I was) with the feeling of speed which only close contact with the ground or clouds produces. Then a sharp climb back to prescribed height and home.

Probably the greatest pleasure of all came with the knowledge that we were handling, on our own, a big, beautiful flying machine which had proven to be the finest bomber in the European Theatre of War. Especially when we acquired our very own G - George, pride of ownership, at least temporarily, helped to lessen some of the nervous strain of operations.

Strange sightings, some of them unexplained, often intrigued us as we flew by night over Continental Europe. Lights on the ground which seemed to keep pace and direction with our flight were among the unexplained phenomena we noticed. We speculated that they were perhaps a system of indicating to German night fighters the path that the bomber stream was following. Although an arrangement of this sort did not seem likely we never did hear any explanation for the mystery lights.

On one night trip we actually saw a German V2 rocket being launched. Although we couldn't see the projectile, the thick smoke trail that followed it high into the sky was clearly visible. The V2s were another of the German schemes to attempt to demoralize the British people, particularly in London. The trajectory of the big rockets could be set so that they would rise to a tremendous height, then gradually level out before plunging downwards and striking a target such as London. The rocket's payload was a heavy concentration of high explosive which devastated a large area when it struck. There was no warning sound before the impact.

"Scarecrows", one or two of which we saw, were an interesting attempt by the Germans to demoralize bomber crews approaching a night target. Fired by an anti-aircraft gun, when they exploded with a fire and smoke effect, the scarecrows were supposed to fool aircrews into thinking that one of their bombers had been hit and destroyed. They weren't a bad attempt at fakery but did not look quite like what they were supposed to portray.

About half way through our tour somebody apparently liked the way we were handling our operations. One day the flight commander called me into his office and said, "How would you like to join P.F.F.?" These initials stood for Pathfinder Force and, coming out of the blue, the query was rather startling. P.F.F. was considered an elite force. From their midst Master Bombers were chosen who "bossed" the operations. They kept a close scrutiny of the target area often from a low height from which they could gauge the effect and the accuracy of the bombing. If they weren't satisfied they could call for target indicator flares, dropped by other Pathfinders, to be shifted to a new position. Then they would call the bomber crews to line up their sights on the new flares.

Certain Pathfinder crews marked the target under the direction of the Master Bomber and other back-up crews continued to add flares when required. Pathfinders were a prestigious lot and it was, we felt, an honour and compliment on our performance as a bomber crew to receive the invitation. We talked it over and decided that if we managed to complete a regular tour we would be doing well. A Pathfinder tour consisted of 50 trips which seemed like starting all over again. So we said, "Thanks, but no thanks" and continued to slug away with 12 Squadron.

JACK E. THOMPSON

We managed to miss an operation one day. We had been assigned to do an air test on a Lancaster that had been repaired. This consisted mainly of the engineer keeping a close watch on his dials and noting anything unusual and also general test of the aircraft's handling and performance. I decided to make the most of this opportunity and turn it into a pleasure trip. So I got Arnold to give me a course for York. I had in mind trying to locate Allerton Park, half way between York and Harrogate and the headquarters for 6 Group, Bomber Command, the Canadian group.

My wife Dorothy was stationed there serving with the Royal Canadian Air Force as a teleprinter operator. We had been married just over four months before in a little village church near Harrogate and I had visited the drafty old castle at Allerton Park on several occasions.

We reached York and I followed the road until I spotted the castle and we proceeded to circle it fairly low, but not too low, so we wouldn't get into trouble.

We headed back for Wickenby and arrived to find a busy station with an operation scheduled which we should have flown. The station had sent out a wireless recall but we had been having too good a time and missed it. The skipper of the crew who replaced us at the last minute was not happy, but at least he had one more to chalk up.

Towards the end of our time on the squadron, and I suppose because we were a senior crew, we were called upon to conduct a very interesting experiment. This was to work with a new device which was used by the navigator in conjunction with his radar equipment. The new equipment provided a method of blind-flying an aircraft during an approach in minimal visibility right down to the end of the runway. F/L Landon, deputy flight commander, acted as check pilot and look-out while I was "under the hood" and only able to see my instruments. Arnold, working the equipment, gave me instructions as to headings and height. We tried it several times and, when Arnold became familiar with the technique it worked like a charm. We never did hear whether it had been adopted for use but at least we had the satisfaction of proving its worth.

Although the standard tour of operations consisted of 30 trips we actually set out on 32 trips but two of them didn't count. On one we didn't reach the target and on the other one we went all the way but circumstances prevented us from bombing.

On what would have been our tenth operation we were briefed for a night trip to Aire in occupied France. By this time, takeoff between the rows of lights which appeared to converge way down at the end of the long runway, was routine. We eventually gained flying speed, the Lanc pulled away from the cling of tarmac, and we roared along parallel to the ground until we reached our climbing speed of 150 MPH. It was shortly after we had gained about 1,000 feet, that the familiar routine was interrupted. Ron told me, "The port outer is over revving. I've got to shut it down." And so he did and so we found ourselves on three engines instead of the accustomed four. He explained that the constant speed unit controlling the propellers had failed. Allowing the three-bladed prop to continue spinning at high speed out of control could result in a blade flying off and slicing through the fuselage.

I quickly trimmed the rudders to compensate for the pull towards the left; Ron feathered the propeller. This was a necessary procedure to reduce the drag of three propeller blades with their flat sides interrupting the airflow. Feathering turned the blades at right angles so just their thin edges cut through the air flowing past.

There was no problem as far as staying aloft was concerned. Lancs flew very well on three engines and even maintained height for a considerable distance on two. But we did have a basic problem. We were carrying a full bomb load and a heavy petrol load. We were at 1,000 feet and our assigned height at the target was 18,000 feet. There was no way we were going to be able to climb to even a reasonable height and get to the target in time on three engines. I could picture us cruising along all alone over Aire long after the bomber force had set course for home. We would be at the mercy of all the ack-ack batteries and any night fighters around the area.

It didn't take long to make the decision. We aborted the operation and headed for the North Sea to dispose of our load. When we arrived back at Wickenby about an hour and a half later we requested permission to fly a right-hand circuit following the rule of always turning towards a live engine.

S/L Carrie, the flight commander, drove out to see us at dispersal and I reported what had happened. His gung-ho comment was, "Well, you've got to stick your neck out sometime!" and he drove away.

As far as I was concerned we were sticking our necks out on every trip even with all the equipment in full working order. I thought, and I still think, it was much better to preserve an aircraft and crew to fly another day rather than adopting the "press on regardless" philosophy of some. Perhaps we made up for this seeming lack of total commitment in his eyes on the later trip to Cologne with a useless rear turret, but that is a story for the next chapter.

The other trip which didn't count towards our 30 added three hours and forty minutes to our log book totals but achieved nothing else. We were heading for a target in the Calais area, flying over a full overcast. I don't know whether the meteorologists expected the cloud to break up by our time of arrival but it remained, an impenetrable blanket hiding the target area.

The Master Bomber's decision was to abort the operation and cart our bombs back home. We had never landed with as much weight aboard and certainly not with a cargo of high explosives. It was with some anxiety that we approached the runway and dropped fairly heavily but with no ill effects.

One other time we almost missed a trip. It was one we wouldn't have minded missing but this was not to be. As we were trundling down the runway, throttles wide open, Chappy suddenly called out, "Tommy, I can see petrol running out onto the port wing!" I took a quick glance out the side window and, sure enough, a liquid spray was gusting across a portion of the wing area. I chopped the throttles and we turned off the runway at an intersection and taxied to a hardstand where we shut down the motors.

Within minutes ground crew were busily looking for the problem, perhaps a loose filler cap. At any rate we were given the go-ahead and any idea of a night off was cancelled as we made our way once more to the end of the runway.

Aircraft recognition had been drummed into all of us with great thoroughness during our training. The ground school subject was considered so important that we pilots were threatened with expulsion from further training if we didn't score at least 95 per cent on our final examination. So we spent endless hours identifying silhouettes which were flashed on a screen at varying speeds up to a fraction of a second.

In spite of this intensive exposure it was difficult to make a rapid decision as to aircraft type on a very dark night when the machine in question was little more than a darker shadow in the gloom. One night a twin-engined Mosquito came dangerously close to being fired on by our gunners as its pilot guided the aircraft past us heading in the same direction. Cal started to call a warning to me, then at the last minute, made identification before opening fire. There were several twin-engined fighters in the Luftwaffe including the Messerschmitt 110, 210 and 410 and the Junkers 88, all of which were dangerous to encounter.

Naval gunners were, on the whole, suspicious of aircraft, so it was no great surprise to us to find we were being fired upon one night as we flew over one of the beach areas where a D-Day landing had been made. The bit of flak that came our way was not too impressive but Chappy fired off the colours of the day anyway from the Verey pistol provided for such situations. I can't remember whether they stopped firing after that or whether they pumped up a few more rounds just to keep in practice. But we were well away before any possible damage could result and had a laugh at being fired upon by our supposed friends.

Ron Smith, flight engineer

CHAPTER 12

It would be boring for a reader to learn the details of all of our trips. Suffice it to say, there was a great sameness to flying each operation in terms of preparation, takeoff, cruising along, dropping our bombs and returning home. At the same time there was something different about almost every trip that separates it in our minds from the others. I propose therefore, to describe highlights and incidents that occurred during a number of our operations.

For the first sixteen trips of the tour we flew a variety of Lancasters, some once, some several times. On a couple of occasions we were assigned G - George which was to become our own aircraft for the last half of the tour. When we received our own aeroplane it was with a feeling of pride. We had completed sixteen operations against the enemy and were now considered an experienced crew. We felt more as though we were accepted members of the squadron and not transients undergoing a test to see if we were fit to belong.

Several of the trips which led up to this half-way mark in our tour provided some interesting, sometimes exciting memories. An early August daylight trip to Trossy St. Maximin in France took us much longer than expected and I'm sure we were the last Lancaster to straggle back over the English Channel on the return flight.

On the way out I noted that the aircraft was pulling badly to port and one of the green lights indicating "wheels down and locked" was showing on the panel. One of the big undercarriage wheels had dropped from its locked up position and was hanging, causing a lot of drag.

I trimmed the aircraft to make allowance and had no difficulty controlling our direction. When it came time to select "bomb doors open" nothing happened. So Ron, being right on the ball, gave a shot of emergency air which I didn't know existed until then, the doors opened and we were able to drop our load. Another shot of compressed air closed the doors and we were on our way home.

We couldn't do a thing about the hanging wheel which was causing a great loss of air speed. We began to feel very much alone and very exposed in the great expanse of blank sky as the last of the Lancasters disappeared ahead of us. Talk about a "sitting duck" situation! All we needed was a German fighter to spot us and we would be in a desperate predicament.

A fighter did spot us and slid into close formation on our port side, the pilot giving us a friendly wave. There were no black crosses but rather colourful roundels of the RAF on the fuselage of this most famous of British fighters, a Spitfire. We were very happy for this protection as we dragged our way back across the Channel and on to our aerodrome. The Spitfire stayed right with us until we were circling Wickenby before the pilot waved goodbye and banked away. We managed to get the starboard wheel down and locked without much trouble. With the undercarriage lever selected to the down position, I put the Lanc into a short, sharp dive ending with a quick pull-out. The centrifugal force generated by the sudden up-thrust forced the wheel down and it thunked into place nicely giving us the second green indicator on the instrument panel.

It was sometime later that a newspaper account told of the extreme heroism of a Canadian pilot at Trossy St. Maximin. Squadron Leader I.W. Bazalgette, DFC of Calgary was Master Bomber for the operation. His aircraft was hit and set on fire but he was able to mark the target and ensure the success of the raid. He ordered those of his crew who could to bail out and then tried to save the lives of his wounded bomb aimer and mid-upper gunner who was overcome by fumes. He attempted a landing near a French village but the aircraft exploded as he touched down. S/L Bazalgette was awarded the Victoria Cross posthumously.

On another daylight raid two days after our fighter-escorted return to base we flew to Blaye in the south of France to destroy an oil refinery. This was a very long eight hours and fifteen minutes bit of flying. We flew very low out over the south-western tip of England over Land's End, skirted France's Brest Peninsula and then across the Bay of Biscay to the target area. We had been briefed to stay at 100 feet above the surface on this long sea crossing so German radar could not pick us up. The Bay of Biscay was noted for the large number of Junkers 88 fighters deployed in its vicinity.

Flying this low above the monotonous surging sea, a pilot had to be careful not to become mesmerized. At least one pilot was either not careful enough or else decided to do some extremely low flying. We saw the aircraft strike the water and vanish.

Upon arriving back over England, Chappy received a message that we were being diverted to Church Broughton because Wickenby was fogged in. This, coming on the heels of a long, tiring flight was bad news but at least we had an airport at which to make a safe landing. Church Broughton was an Australian operational training unit.

The next morning, taking off for our home station, we got a real kick out of giving the still-in-training Aussies something to see. The Lancs were light, a small fuel load and no bombs, so with full throttle settings for takeoff we literally sprang into the air. Then each aircraft in turn sped along the downwind leg (opposite to takeoff direction), banked down over the end of the runway, and zoomed along its length at a couple of hundred feet, pulling up at the end in a showy steep climbing turn. It was a strictly spontaneous farewell to our hosts and a thrill for us to show off in our big operational machines. Boys will be boys and, after all, we were still pretty young!

The German city of Brunswick received our attention on the night of August 12th. This target gave a real example of our attitude towards the job, to give it our best.

The sky over Brunswick, when we arrived, was a horrendous nightmare with the usual searchlights, flak bursts, smoke and the condensation trails of numerous night fighters illuminated by the flames and flashes from the ground. We were cranked up to full tension as we started our bomb run, Jim giving me the usual "Left" and "Right" directions. Then our bomb aimer suddenly interrupted his terse instructions with, "No good. We'll have to go around again." It was like a bad dream hearing his words. Just when we felt we were going to drop the load and get out of this boiling cauldron Jim's message shattered our hopes.

Well, there was no question about it, we would indeed have to orbit this hot-bed of flak and fighters and make another run. We never doubted Jim's decision. He knew that his bombs were not going to find the right target so there was no other course of action. I'm sure he felt just as worried about sticking our necks out by hanging around this hotly contested aerial battleground as the rest of us.

So we circled around Brunswick and once more settled into the bombing run. On most occasions the Messerschmitts and Focke Wulfes seemed to shy away from the target area when the anti-aircraft fire was heavy. But the contrails announced their presence. Jim, at one time, reported a fighter crossing at right angles about 500 feet below our nose. We were flying the straight and level bombing run at the time and held our concerted breaths hoping the pilot wouldn't look up, and apparently he didn't. So we dropped our load and really got out of there!

A relatively simple but interesting operation occurred one morning when we set forth to bomb Cap Gris Nez. This point on the French coast lay just 20 miles across the Strait of Dover from England. Well fortified huge coastal guns rained death and destruction on the English port city of Dover and also could be trained on convoys sailing the intervening waterway. We were pleased to have a chance to help silence those behemoths of destruction.

We were flying over ten-tenths cloud which continued to show no sign of dispersing and would completely mask the target. Suddenly over the r/t came instructions from the Master Bomber, "Get down under the cloud". Almost as one, Lancs on each side of us and ahead throttled back, dropped their undercarriages and flaps in order to descend as quickly as possible at a reduced speed. The angle of descent can be surprisingly steep when the obstructions to the air flow are brought into play.

We all disappeared into the cloud looking like a flock of hawks diving with talons extended ready to pounce on their prey. We levelled out just under the cloud base at 3,000 feet and bombed from that altitude, six times lower than our average bombing height.

The steel works at the industrial giant of Duisburg, Germany provided us with our one and only double-header.

A daylight trip to that city had proven to be unsuccessful. We didn't learn why this was but gathered that the follow-up photo reconnaissance showed the target still alive and producing. Whether the Pathfinder Force and Master Bomber had boobed in their target marking or whether the bomber force had been less than efficient we didn't know.

But, regardless of the cause, we attended a briefing for the same target just a few hours after we had arrived back at base. Ours not to reason why, etc. Just back to the briefing but and an eventual five plus more hours of flying on the same day.

During the earlier flight to Duisburg our squadron had a special guest aboard one of its aircraft. Richard Dimbleby, top news reporter for the BBC, whose cultured, sonorous tones were familiar to millions in Britain, went along for the ride. Our aircraft, G - George by this time, was not chosen to host the famous correspondent. Nevertheless we felt honoured that our squadron from among many, had been chosen for this special recognition.

Unfortunately this particular operation was not the auspicious occasion it might have been but I'm sure Mr. Dimbleby did not recognize this at the time. We didn't hear the broadcast but it's likely that the veteran correspondent gave Bomber Command a good pat on the back. At any rate, although we would much rather have had a good night's sleep, we were on the way back to give Duisburg another pasting and to vindicate ourselves.

As we flew out over England, Chappy picked up some dance music on the radio, likely Giraldo or Glenn Miller, and the sound of swing wafting from our head-sets made that part of the journey less gruelling. A news broadcast that followed quoted German radio as stating that a large concentration of bombers was enroute from England and heading towards Germany. It was rather startling to hear ourselves being described over enemy radio almost before we were well on our way towards the target.

I don't remember a great deal about this trip. We returned to the scene of our former debacle and, this time, pranged the target properly. We heard no more about Duisburg and never flew there again although I'm sure there were many other operations to that target before the war ended.

Out of our 32 trips almost one-quarter of them were to "Happy Valley". We were fortunate. Many other crews logged a much higher percentage to this infamous piece of German territory.

"Happy Valley" was the aircrew designation for the Ruhr Valley, the heart of German industrial might and so, naturally, prime target territory for Allied bomber forces. The sobriquet of "Happy Valley" was, of course, a reversal of the valley's true nature. Being the prime source for sorely-needed steel and equipment for the armed forces of Germany, its importance to the country could not be over-exaggerated. So the Ruhr bristled with defences ringing its cities and industrial complexes. Flak "thick enough to walk on" filled the skies whenever bomber forces trespassed through the Valley's air space. Whether by day or night, thousands of anti-aircraft guns threatened to extinguish the lives of aircrew ordered to the Ruhr. The losses of men and aircraft were, at times, heavy.

Our trips to "Happy Valley" included, of course, Duisburg, a couple to Essen, a visit to Neuss and the last two operations of our tour, to Bochum and Gelsenkirchen. The latter was described in Chapter 1.

The city of Cologne, south of the Ruhr Valley in Germany, was singled out by the powers that be in Bomber Command for three visits in four days in late October. The crew of G - George was among the invited guests who participated in all three aerial assaults.

It was getting very close to the end of our tour, during those dangerous last five trips in fact, that the Cologne raids took place. And we were a little bit on the twitchy side knowing the next several trips would make or break us.

The first raid, a daylight, I barely recollect, although this was the furthest penetration into Germany we had made in daylight hours. But I, and I'm sure the other crew members, have no difficulty in recalling Cologne by night. The first of our worries was that a full moon was making a mockery of night flying as we knew it. This beautiful but deadly moon was providing the finest illumination any night fighter pilot could want, even if he hadn't been eating his carrots!

To make matters worse Cal had called up early in the trip when we were barely over the continent to announce that his rear turret was out of action. It was caused by hydraulic failure. Cal could swing the turret very slowly by hand and fire one burst from his four guns after which we had no firepower left, just the lesser protection from Jonesy's mid-upper guns.

What a situation! The thought of travelling hundreds of miles without the rear turret in operation was a daunting one. But certain extra risks had to be accepted at times and we carried on. I'm sure the effect on Cal must have been almost unbearable. To have to sit in his turret, a very vulnerable position, and be unable to respond to an attack with anything more than a short burst. What a few tense hours he must have spent!

We must have been in one of the later waves because I remember seeing bombers far below us, glinting in the moonlight as they returned from the target. One such sight was etched clearly on my memory, a Messerschmitt 110 or 210 banking behind a Lancaster to carry out a diving curve-of-pursuit attack. The two aircraft passed behind us out of sight very quickly so I don't know what resulted. But the vivid image of the two aircraft is frozen in my mind like a slide projected on a screen, a dramatically frightening picture of aerial warfare.

Fortunately we managed to sneak along through that cursedly brilliant sky without attracting attention for which we were very thankful.

One of the chief dreads of bomber crews was to be picked up by those waving fingers of light, the searchlights which were part of the defences of most major targets.

These beams, which were powerful enough to illuminate aircraft at 20,000 feet and more, waved around through the sky in an apparently aimless manner. Actually they were waiting until some hapless bomber was seized from the darkness by a radar-controlled master beam, blue in colour. Immediately this beam locked on to the aircraft, it was joined by all of the other searchlights positioned around the target area and the unlucky aircraft was "coned". This was an apt description for the display of beams which started on a broad base and ended in a narrow point where all the light paths converged.

An aeroplane caught in these brilliant beams appeared, at a distance, like a tiny moth unable to resist the beckoning flame.

We had seen a number of bombers coned during our tour and were always hopeful that we could evade the grasping white fingers. There were two good reasons for wanting to retain the anonymity of a dark sky around us. An illuminated bomber provided a nice target for a night fighter and, once the searchlights were locked on, anti-aircraft fire could be pumped up the beams with great accuracy.

So it was a sudden and shocking situation for us when the master beam locked on G - George over Bochum and its many cohorts swung in to bathe us in such brilliance that we were completely blinded. We had heard of the extreme difficulty of breaking away once the beams had caught their prey. My immediate and automatic reaction was to bank sharply and dive and, much to my surprise, we slipped from the clutches of this dazzling, evil luminescence within a few seconds.

What a relief was that cloak of darkness into which we fled! The incident had happened at the beginning of our bomb run so we quickly got back on track and carried on with the job at hand.

It was months later, while talking to a friend in my home town, that I learned his younger brother had been shot down over Bochum that same night.

The coning at Bochum and the close call when a nearby Lanc had exploded at Gelsenkirchen made it seem as if the Old Reaper had decided we had got off too easily during our previous 30 trips and tried desperately to right the situation at the last moment. But luck was on our side. We cheated him.

Our taste of war was over with those final two trips into Happy Valley and we were satisfied that we had acquitted ourselves well and happy that we managed to escape unscathed. The passing of time has a way of making the desperate seem less desperate, the fear less fearful. It is impossible, more than 40 years after these events, to summon up the feeling of fear which I'm sure we all often felt and the flood of relief after it was all over. But I know, we all know, the crew of G - George, that way back then it was all very real.

THE END

JACK E. THOMPSON

Jack and Dorothy on the River Nid, Knaresborough, Yorkshire, on their wedding day, April 29, 1944

EPILOGUE

Well, the foregoing pages are an ancient bit of modern history. At this writing the events I have described took place 45 years ago. And yet, much of what happened to us then, is as clear in my mind as the photograph I have of our crew standing behind the rear turret of G - George.

By chance, we were born at the right time to play roles in the greatest conflict in the world's history. By chance, from among the 100,000 aircrew who flew in Bomber Command, we seven were thrown together. And, by chance, ours turned out to be a good combination.

Years after the war, we discovered through published statistics that we had had a less than 50 per cent chance of survival. Only 40,000 out of the 100,000 members of Bomber Command aircrew came through and not all of those in one piece. Many bear physical scars as souvenirs of their war. We, on the other hand, came back unscarred and with a host of indelibly imprinted memories which sometimes seem more like a fantastic dream than a reality.

The crew who flew our own G - George (LM213) on a trip on January 16, 1945 was not so fortunate. George failed to return on that date, its 64th operation. Three other Lancasters we flew were also lost. Z-Zebra (LM1O7) failed to come back from an operation on July 28, 1944, nine days after we had been assigned to it for a training flight. Another training flight, this time in L-Love (ND699), was carried out just 24 days before that aircraft was lost. A new Love carried us on an operation to the

French port of Le Havre on September 5th. This aircraft disappeared about four and one-half months later.

One of the Lancasters we flew, N-Nan (ME758), had the distinction of being retired after completing 108 operations, all with 12 Squadron. A charmed ship indeed!

On the occasion of our first reunion in 1985 we were surprised to receive awards from the Netherlands Government. Their ambassador in Ottawa, Jan Breman, read about the reunion from an interview with Chappy published in the *Ottawa Citizen*. Mr. Breman immediately sent a letter and six medals to Chappy. The letter in part read:

> ...The news caption mentioned operations in the Arnhem area which allows me to relate this Embassy to your reunion.
>
> ...You may have known that this year (1985) a great number of Canadian veterans visited my country on a very special pilgrimage on which occasion those present were given, as a token of gratitude and remembrance, the Erasmus Medal. It would be a great honour for me if you were to accept this medal for yourself and members of the crew of G - George at your reunion, as a token of appreciation and warm friendship which united us all on those dark nights.

Needless to say we, the crew of G - George were honoured and pleased with this surprise presentation. Since most of the veterans who travelled to the Netherlands for the liberation remembrance were Army, it is unlikely that many air crew veterans are recipients of the Erasmus Medal.

After we five Canadians returned from overseas we learned that our crew had received three decorations. Our navigator, Arnold, was awarded the Distinguished Flying Medal (DFM) and we were justly proud that his fine abilities had been so recognized. Jim and I received Distinguished Flying Crosses (DFC). As far as my decoration was concerned I felt that I was receiving it on behalf of the whole crew, all of whom deserved it as much as I did, particularly since it was not awarded for any specific occurrence.

When we returned to civvy street all seven of us had greatly varied occupations.

Jack Chapman, wireless operator/air gunner, although he had always derided his crew mates in friendly fashion as "crazy Canadians", must nevertheless, have acquired a fascination for Canada. After returning to the retail fur business following the war, it was only a few years later in 1954 that he and family emigrated to this country. He and Doreen and children spent 15 years in Winnipeg before moving to Ottawa. There he became president of Burkholder Furs and retired in 1984. Jack and Doreen keep up an active life of sports and enjoy part of each winter in Florida.

Arnold Cowan, navigator, returned to his wife Florence and the pharmaceutical business in Edmonton. He worked for a large drug company as a district representative and retired at age 65. He spent several subsequent years as a dispensing pharmacist until a stroke forced him to retire totally. Arnold and Florence enjoy a month in Hawaii each winter, escaping the frigid Edmonton weather.

Rear-gunner Cal Dagg returned to Sarnia and joined Canadian Customs after he was retired from the RCAF. He married Dot and the couple always lived in Sarnia. For many years Cal was on duty on the Sarnia bridge. Every so often someone from Parry Sound would pass on a "hello" to me from Cal after meeting him as they returned from a visit to the U.S.A. In later years our "gung-ho" gunner was attached to Customs Intelligence and worked with local police, provincial police, RCMP and U.S. Customs on investigations. Apparently Cal had some exciting times. He and Dot also travelled to Europe where he served for a short time as a Customs official with Canadian Armed Forces in Germany.

Gerald Jones, mid-upper gunner, married Jean and the couple have always lived in the Chatham area. Jonesy, who joined the RCAF out of Grade 10 before he was 17½ (said he couldn't wait), met Cal on a gunnery course in England. After the war he spent 30 years with International Harvester retiring as a group leader in the painting department. He and Jean have been wintering in Texas since his retirement.

JACK E. THOMPSON

Our group of seven Bomber Command veterans was sadly reduced to six in 1962 when Jim Peacock, bomb aimer, died of cancer. Dr. James Peacock, DFC, was a successful dental surgeon working in Brantford. He was president of the Brant County Dental Society and secretary of the Brant County branch of the Ontario Dental Association. Jim was married to Aylene and the couple had two children.

Flight engineer Ron Smith was the only one of us who made post-war flying a career. Ron, who is unmarried and lives near Manchester, England, acquired ground engineer and flight engineer licences in 1949 as well as a private pilot's licence. He began his career aboard converted Halifax tankers on the Berlin Airlift and then moved on to a company handling freight charters to many parts of the world. He was involved in the crash of a Halifax at Dum Dum, Calcutta, in which two were killed. He joined BOAC and made flights all over the world aboard Constellations; Stratocruisers, Britannias, Comets, VC 10s and 747s for 30 years. Ron continues to live in England and for some years has been looking after an invalid sister.

The author worked for a short time as a reporter/photographer for his hometown daily, the *Peterborough Examiner*. Another short span with the Department of Lands and Forests led to his settling with his wife Dorothy in Parry Sound. There they operated a photography business for over 20 years. For the following 15 years he served as editor of the Parry Sound *North Star* and retired in 1988. They live on the shores of Georgian Bay where they swim and boat but look forward to many days of downhill skiing. Photography continues to be both hobby and avocation.

Some idea of the close bond which is formed among a group of men who have faced danger together and have been dependent upon one another's skills for their safety is evidenced by the fact that we are still in contact. Christmas cards and the odd letter passed back and forth through the years. And most of us saw one another at some time, although not as a complete group. I just saw Jim Peacock once when he called in while travelling to North Bay. But, thanks to Cal who persisted through much letter writing and phone calls, we held a reunion in 1985 and one in 1988.

These were remarkable events considering that Ron had to travel from England and Arnold from Edmonton. It may well be a very unusual record for an almost intact bomber crew to be reunited after more than 40 years.

Another reunion is currently being planned and indications are that it will be held. So the crew of G - George will once again greet each other and reminisce about those long-ago days when we had our Great Adventure.

REMEMBRANCE

We were not always old, we who stand here shivering not only from November cold but also from our memory-fraught pilgrimage before this grey forbidding shrine.

Our hands were not always veined and wrinkled, our heads not always balding or silver-clad, our bodies not always slow to obey.

We did not always feel the piercing chill as we feel it today, standing in our blue-clad ranks, medals on our chests, as we contemplate the cold and lifeless stone we face.

But here we are in our remaining numbers remembering ....

We're remembering Tommy, Roly, Jim, Gord or a score of other friends not with us today -- all of them in the vibrant flush of youth when we saw them last.

They did not grow old among us to join with us on this day of remembering.

Tommy's years were cut short in Italy when his personnel carrier struck a land mine.

Roly's exuberant youth ceased as his Spitfire spiralled down in flames.

Jim's final moments were spent in cold Atlantic waters after his corvette slipped bow-high beneath the waves.

Gord was caught in a burst of cannon fire from a Focke Wulfe fighter whose pilot concentrated his aim on the rear turret of a Lancaster bomber.

They and thousands like them had left the safe sanctuaries of home, had bid a careless farewell, little thinking that this last glimpse of smiling confidence would be the only legacy left to their loved ones. They headed forth in the bright innocence of youth to help rid the world of the pestilence that threatened to engulf it.

Their innocence of youth was short-lived.

Some quickly learned of the dread scourge beneath the Atlantic waves.

Others crawled through the hell of swarming flies, shimmering heat, scouring grit of blowing sand and a relentless enemy in North Africa.

Still others stumbled through the fierce concentration of fire laid down by the defenders of Dieppe or lay in mud holes shaken by the mind-numbing bombardment of Anzio.

There were others, thousands of them, who slammed through the waves of a wildly-pitching English Channel to help liberate Europe from the oppressors on those early June days of 1944.

Many who survived the withering fire on the French beaches were later to become casualties as the final months of the great struggle ground the foe to a halt.

Those whose youthful innocence quickly fled, numbered among them the many who had heard the battle call and chose to answer it among the clouds.

The flak-ridden, fighter-infested darkness shielded their young eyes from the many horrors below their wings until, suddenly, they were singled out for their own few moments of terror.

The wheeling fighters locked in mortal combat high above their earth-bound brothers, sent the defeated spinning downward, the finality of their flights affirmed by the spiralling signature of black smoke.

These were the young men who, like ourselves, who were also young men, went forth shining-eyed, their minds filled with heroic thoughts.

We returned.

They did not.

We remember them well.

First printed for Remembrance Day, November 11, 1988 in the Parry Sound *North Star*.

JACK E. THOMPSON

EDITOR'S NOTES

I have tried to present my father's story in his own words with only minor changes from the first edition for easier story flow. Primarily, I have digitized the existing photographs and provided others that were not available for the previous edition. I also provided a new cover design and, I hope, have produced a clean type by using Bookman Antiqua fonts throughout.

These events happened to my father and his crew. This is their story. Similar things happened to many other aircrews. They sometimes describe their own experiences as mundane, but we now know that more than 60% of aircrew personnel did not survive to complete their missions.

Fred Cahoon of Severn Bridge, Ontario recently gave me this letter written to him by my father in July 1995, after Fred had read the 1989 book. I think it provides a few more personal details and hints that survival may not have preoccupied the crew but was definitely on their minds.

Dear Fred

What a surprise to receive your letter regarding my book. I am pleased that Steve loaned it to you and that you enjoyed it.

I think that anyone who has been in some branch of the service enjoys books on service life be it navy, army, air force or what-have-you.

Our crew was a lucky one. You never knew when you "crewed up" at a moment's notice how things would work between you and how competent each person would be. I had no worries on that score.

And we were lucky on our trips. Mind you, we flew at a less dangerous time than in the earlier years. We had excellent equipment including radar, the best heavy bomber in the world and a decent time period, weather-wise. We did not fly through winter storms and fog.

I was particularly pleased when Arnold, our navigator, received the Distinguished Flying Medal. The medals were awarded to NCOs, the crosses to officers. And the medals were much less common, just a few hundred awarded. Since the award was not for a single courageous act, it must recognize his expertise as a navigator. We felt that he was particularly good at his job and greatly improved our chances of success and survival.

I don't remember the "Twelve O'clock High" TV series you mentioned but I have a taped copy of the movie starring Gregory Peck as commanding officer. It's pretty down to earth and not "Hollywoodish" and an excellent picture. Be glad to loan it to you if you are interested.

I have read several books based on modern aircraft carrier flying and am very glad I was not involved in any of that hairy business.

I have a friend who flew a Seafire, the naval version of the Spitfire, off carriers in the far east in the British Fleet Air Arm. Hope to get him talking about it.

So Fred, all for now and thanks for reading my little book and writing to me about it.

As a child of about six, I had met both Ron Smith and Cal Dagg. Even though I did not meet any other members of the bomber crew until 1991, all their names were well known to me. Neither of my parents spoke very much about their wartime experiences; however, the names of the crew members were very well known to me as important, almost mythic people.

My parents, Jack and Dorothy Thompson, both served in the wartime RCAF. They met in Halifax, then again in Shrewsbury, Shropshire many weeks later through the magic of love. My father spent his operational time flying from Wickenby, while my mother was based mainly at 6 Group Headquarters at Allerton Hall, near Knaresborough in Yorkshire.

On April 29, 1944, Jack and Dorothy were married in a small church in the village of Green Hammerton in Yorkshire. In April 2005, my wife Donna and I traveled with my sister Andrea and brother-in-law Merv to Green Hammerton and many places in England and Scotland that paralleled the travel of our parents during WWII. Sixty-one years later, to the day, April 29, 2005, we visited that same church. The church was locked, but through the welcoming assistance of friendly villagers, we were able to enter and visit the church.

We also visited Shrewsbury, Wickenby, Lincoln, Knaresborough, Allerton Hall, and Edinburgh Castle, all important venues for our parents.

Not much remains at Wickenby although the airport is operating as a commercial airstrip. The original control tower remains as an operations centre, coffee shop and a small museum celebrating the operations of 12 and 626 Squadrons who shared the aerodrome. One thousand eighty aircrew died in operations from the Wickenby airfield.

Since the first printing, my father managed to contact Frank Watt, who is mentioned in the book right from the first chapter. Frank had returned to his home in Argentina following the war and replied to my father's contact letter on March 21, 1992, 48 years after the two pilots parted company in Wickenby.

> Dear Tommy
>
> I can't thank you enough for your letter. To say it would be a complete surprise to me was, of course, a masterful understatement …
>
> Before going any further, I must congratulate you on the book, because of all the "war books" I have read over the years, yours is the most faithful reproduction of what a bomber crew went through, just as it was, with no heroics or special embellishments but with the overall feeling that everything was stacked against us and the probability of survival, to put it mildly, was remote …

Frank went on to quote research results he was privy to that for the operations period while they were both at Wickenby, the losses were 76% for a tour of about 30 trips.

> In other words, one crew out of four walked out through the gate they came in by. A sobering thought indeed …

Jack and Dorothy were able to get together with Frank and Sylvia Watt shortly after this initial correspondence when the Watts visited their two adult children who had immigrated to Canada in the 1970s. During the ensuing ten years, there were several more reunions, especially after the senior Watts also immigrated.

In September 2004, we Thompson children and our spouses joined our mother, Dorothy, to journey to Vancouver from Ontario to finally meet the Watts, their children and families. In one of life's wonderful outcomes, amazingly, the next generation of two pilot friends bonded instantly.

The Author

Jack Thompson was born and raised in Peterborough, Ontario, then lived with his wife, Dorothy, for 57 years in Parry Sound, Ontario.

The Editor

Steve Thompson is Jack Thompson's son, was born in Toronto but was raised in Parry Sound. He now lives with his wife on the edge of the Carden Plain near Kirkfield, Ontario.

Printed in the United States
99189LV00003B/275/A